LOVE HURTS

Love Hurts

Helen Sinclair
with
Melanie Symonds

HODDER AND STOUGHTON
LONDON SYDNEY AUCKLAND

Helen Sinclair has gifted all her proceeds from this book to Topsy's Children for the medical centre in Iasi.

Extracts from *Leukaemia in Children* (1991, © Leukaemia Research Fund, are reproduced by kind permission of the Leukaemia Research Fund, 43, Great Ormond Street, London, WC1N 3JJ.

Unless otherwise indicated, Scripture quotations are taken from the New King James Version. Other quotations are from the HOLY BIBLE, NEW INTERNATIONAL VERSION, copyright © 1973, 1978, 1984, by the International Bible Society. Used by permission.

A CIP cataloguing record for this title is available from the British Library.

ISBN 0 340 57617 0

Typeset by Hewer Text Composition Services, Edinburgh
Printed and bound in Great Britain by
Cox & Wyman Ltd, Reading, Berks.

Hodder and Stoughton Ltd
A division of Hodder Headline PLC
47 Bedford Square
London WC1B 3DP

Contents

Foreword

My heart went out to her. She was sitting in my kitchen, her bearing as stately, as undefeated as ever, but with just the hint of a droop about the shoulders.

She was, she said, indescribably weary. The rigours of her one-woman crusade to Romania had been nothing compared to the effect of a boisterous four-year-old suddenly commandeering her life.

I understood all right. Energetic children – and I have several – can strain the nerves like nothing else on earth. In your thirties, with a bit of practice, you can just about cope, but to have a dynamo like Richard Andries land in your living-room and take over your orderly, evenly paced life at the age of sixty-seven is . . . well, it's a shock.

Once again, I had to take my hat off to Helen Sinclair. Those shoulders of hers didn't sag for long. God, she reckoned, would somehow give her the strength to cope with being tickled every time she tried to have a nap. That boy needed her, she had taken him on, she would get through the days somehow. And she did.

Hers is the most indomitable spirit I have ever encountered. Once the bit is between her teeth, there is no stopping her; and woe betide anyone who tries. There is about her still the spirit of the girl who grew up in the New Zealand bush, riding ten miles to school every day in all weathers, chiselling the snow from the horse's shoes.

The effect of Helen in full, tenacious flight has been known to devastate the faint-hearted. She is someone who likes, as she says herself, to 'speak her mind'.

But as Richard Andries and so many of his Romanian compatriots know, she has a heart as soft as jelly. No, not jelly: Helen Sinclair never wobbles. Nor is she as soft as butter, which is much too drippy. Her heart is as soft as a sponge, absorbing hurts and pains and frustrations, never squeezed dry.

I have watched her over the last few years taking on more and more as the need of the people of Romania gripped her. 'Go easy, Helen,' we would warn her. 'Get yourself well first.' But again and again, she put us all to shame with her insistence that there was a job to be done and it was her calling to do it, angina, bronchitis, gammy leg, or not.

She had next to no money, but that didn't stop her responding to the appeal that brought little Richard to Britain. Just as she used to half-starve herself so that she could feed her beloved dogs on best lambs' livers, so she began systematically to sell some of her most cherished possessions to ensure that Richard and his mother ate well in her home. She literally gave her last penny to pay the international phone bills, the taxis and the thousand and one domestic expenses that came in the wake of her decision to try and save Richard's life.

For the treatment at Great Ormond Street Hospital, she needed frightening amounts of money. It was a tremendous strain on one single elderly lady to know that she and she alone was responsible for finding the £395 a day that it cost to keep him alive. To minimise the bills, she was allowed to nurse him from time to time in her own little flat in Harrow, knowing always that the slightest infection could kill him. And all the time, with no experience of PR or the media, she was having to hustle for publicity and solicit the sort of limelight she hates for herself, in order to keep reaching out to the conscience of the nation.

It was hard, very hard. Yet even when she had done her bit for Richard, she didn't stop. And she hasn't stopped yet. There is still the orphanage and the medical centre that she wants to see built in Romania, still money to raise, vans to buy, architectural plans to discuss, medical supplies to find. Helen pause for breath? Helen take a break? We ought to have known.

What we who love her relish enormously is the gleam it has all brought to Helen's eye. Yes, it takes a lot out of her physically, but it has given her a zest that comes, I think, with knowing how much you can achieve – whatever age you are – if your faith is true and your mind is set on it.

It has taken her into utterly new territory, from family planning to high finance. It certainly makes for diverting conversation. One minute she's regaling us with details of condom supplies for the medical centre, the next with a highly technical assessment of the latest medical wonder-machine. She discusses architectural niceties with aplomb and the vicissitudes of child-rearing with the enhanced understanding of one who has not forgotten what it means to have your sleep ruined and the bathroom flooded.

Over these last years, which she says have been the most precious and useful of her life, her friends have watched her with awe. We have seen in Helen a woman who has followed her God and achieved what seemed impossible. We have watched her blossom.

I think you will enjoy her story.

Sally Magnusson

1

My Romanian Resolution

'I want very mutch save my little son Richard he is three years old.'

I stared at the broken English on the flimsy airmail paper. A foreign woman I had never met was appealing to me, of all people, for help. Her name, she wrote, was Dana Andries and her son Richard had leukaemia. At the moment he was briefly in remission, but drugs and proper treatment were not available in Romania. She knew that we had the right treatment in the West. Without the treatment her son would die. It was as simple as that.

Her next request was direct but hardly straightforward: 'If you are so kind to invite me with my little son to England, please make sure and send to me one invitation of you or from the hospital that to be capable to receave from the english ambossy the visas for both.' Too taken aback to smile at the spelling, I read on.

She enclosed some hospital papers showing her son's blood tests. And she had a little money, enough for the train only – flying by plane would be much too expensive for them.

If it had not been for my experiences in the past year, when I had achieved more than I ever thought possible, I would have sent a polite refusal and my heartfelt sympathy, as well as promising to pray for the little boy. Life was different now, though. I had proved, both to myself and the many well-meaning people who had tried, with the best motives, to discourage me, that an older person with a little determination could overcome minor disabilities –

I walk with a stick and have some arthritis – and achieve the same results as a younger person.

The difference now was that when I received this letter I had already been to Romania and I would have defied anyone with the same experience to refuse to help them. This little boy was not strange or foreign to me. Even though I had not seen his face, I could imagine it, having seen the faces of hundreds of other Romanian children. He might have the security of loving parents, but his suffering was as real as that of the orphans with their listless eyes and shaved heads, who were surprised and delighted if an adult paid them any attention. One could only wonder how they would deal with their past when they grew up.

Such children were not, perhaps, as ill as this little boy, but their needs were as great. And in the same way that I believed God had used me to help one group of children, I now believed He would empower me to help Richard.

When I received the letter from Richard's mother, I had been home from Romania for four months. I knew what conditions were like there and could imagine how the family was living. Nor could I deceive myself about the medical treatment available; hospitals were very poorly equipped. I knew of one hospital which possessed a single syringe for all its injections. And that was a town hospital. In the countryside it was worse: a doctor might be responsible for four or five villages yet could not dispense so much as an aspirin.

Of course I had hoped to recuperate for a time now, but the knowledge of Richard's state made this impossible. Quite clearly, I could see the path marked out for me. A genteel retirement was now a remote, almost laughable prospect. Whether I liked it or not, my future seemed to be inevitably linked to Romania.

After an eventful and much-travelled life I had been settling into retirement, content to look after my little dog. Despite some physical disability, I did not have to rely on anyone and rather enjoyed my quiet independence.

So what had happened to shake me out of my retirement? Simply this: I became convinced that I must do
something to help the people of Romania. As far as I
was concerned, it was a God-given conviction, because
on my own I could never have achieved so much – and
I never expected to see my life change so dramatically!

It all started with the Romanian revolution in December
1989, when the people's struggle for liberation touched a
chord with many of us in other parts of Europe.

We had watched with joy and trepidation as President
Ceauşescu's desperate citizens rose up to overthrow his
brutal regime. In the West we knew of the sufferings
inflicted on Christians – no religious belief was compatible
with Ceauşescu's orthodox Communism – yet even we
were astonished to hear of Christianity's prominence
amidst the turmoil.

It had been a grotesque and intrusive regime. Many
telephones in the country had a built-in microphone linked
to the Securitate, Romania's loathed secret police. A visit
from a foreigner to a pastor guaranteed his subsequent
arrest and interrogation. Our minister knew of one pastor
who was visited by the secret police every day for the past
three years. For an hour or more he would be asked, 'Who
have you spoken to today? What did they say? What did
they want? What did you say to them? What have you been
doing today? What have you been reading? What are you
preparing?'

One young man could recall his father, a pastor, never
going to bed at night without packing a small bag of warm
clothes and leaving it by the door in case 'they' came for
him in the night. Recently opened archives in Timisoara
revealed thousands of files on police informers about
the people they had reported: family members, work
colleagues, church 'brothers and sisters'.

People lived in fear; one pastor called it 'a climate
of suspicion. We didn't know if our own children were
informing on us. In that atmosphere we even feared each
other. We couldn't sleep and we couldn't work.'

Pastor Richard Wurmbrand, whose fourteen-year imprisonment included solitary confinement and torture, had become a legend in Western Christian circles after his enforced expulsion. Some of the deeds of the Securitate during the uprising itself were similarly dreadful; no wonder many of us believed that God in His mercy had delivered that country from the evil in its midst.

So now we hoped the land would find some peace and prosperity. At that stage I think very few Westerners, even those Christians who had been permitted to visit fellow believers during the vicious forty-year dictatorship, were prepared for the sights behind this particular section of the Iron Curtain.

Meanwhile Christmas came. Each year I spent it with my friends, John and Elspeth Raynar, in their glorious old house at Lolworth, just outside Cambridge. After Christmas I was to stay on and 'house sit' for three months while they visited relatives in Australia.

My peaceful break in the country was interrupted by a phone call from London. The minister of my church, Dr John Nicholls, was going to Romania on 1st January with a cargo of Bibles, medical supplies, food and clothes. I was not surprised that a member of the congregation should call me on holiday; as the only evangelical Scottish Presbyterian church in London our congregation is a close one with members travelling long distances to worship near St Paul's every Sunday.

Our interest in Romania was not new; for a number of years members of my church had travelled to the closed countries of Eastern Europe, making many Christian contacts amongst its persecuted churches. Nor was it John's first visit to Romania; fifteen years previously he had helped a group of Christians in Iasi (pronounced 'Yarsh') of whom he had grown very fond. Now he wanted to satisfy himself of their safety amidst the turmoil of the revolution while bringing in medicine and Bibles.

On this occasion, however, I was very concerned; we were being asked to pray for John's safety because a trip to Romania at this time was unpredictable, if not downright dangerous. The weather conditions were said to be dreadful, never mind the risks of entering a country where law and order had broken down.

Our prayers for John's safety were answered; just over three weeks later I received a tape of a sermon he had given on his return. I sat down to listen to it at once – then listened again.

Throughout the trip they had been conscious of God's protection. After some narrow escapes in their driving and several strange experiences (including having their luggage stolen by gipsies and restored by outraged citizens) they saw everything working together for good.

It was these experiences which moved me more than I could ever have expected. John only had time to give us what he called 'a bird's-eye view of a country in upheaval in the midst of a continent in change'. He painted a picture of ordinary people, just like us, blinking in the sunlight of unexpected freedom.

Our Romanian friends simply could not believe what was happening. After years of repression, it was hard to accept freedom overnight. People in the streets felt they were dreaming. This was confirmed by, of all people, a Czech lady interpreter whom John met in Prague's Wenceslas Square on their way home. Psalm 126 was read out:

When the LORD brought back the captives to Zion,
We were like men who dreamed.
Our mouths were filled with laughter,
Our tongues with songs of joy.
Then it was said among the nations,
'The LORD has done great things for them.'
The LORD has done great things for us,
And we are filled with joy. (NIV)

This woman, who made no profession of Christian faith,

exclaimed on hearing the first two lines, 'That's it! That's exactly how we all feel.'

For one elderly couple living in the city of Brasov, the first signs of change came from their television. One day, instead of the endless pictures of Ceauşescu making speeches, scenes of rioting and shooting in Bucharest flashed on to their screen. They watched in uncomprehending silence until the husband said, 'I think it must be a historical film.' Even the appearance of a Liberation Front spokesman failed to persuade them that anything out of the ordinary was happening.

The religious dimension to the Romanian Revolution was undeniable. Of course no one could claim that the revolution was conducted on Christian principles – it was certainly not free from bloodshed – nor were all its proponents Christians. Yet while our Western press had reported the fact that the uprising began with the arrest of a Reformed Church pastor, less attention was given to the nation's spiritual hunger. Oddly enough, it was a small item in the *Independent*'s weekend magazine about burying the dead of the revolution which referred to 'the huge outpouring of Romanian religious feeling, the most striking consequence of the revolution after the downfall of the Ceauşescus'.

Everywhere there was disbelief and wonder at the manner in which their country had been liberated. Even the soldiers confided to John that they would have been powerless to overthrow Ceauşescu on their own because they were deliberately kept short of weapons. Each man was issued with just four bullets; the Securitate held all the ammunition.

Nor was it any coincidence that the revolution broke out in a church. John had stood in the pulpit of the Reformed Church in Timisoara looking down at the very spot where the elders and members had struggled against the Securitate arresting their pastor, Laszlo Tokes, and carrying him away for interrogation and torture. Now the church and the people bore the marks of oppression. A

door below the pulpit had been simply left hanging where it
was ripped away by the accusers. One of the elders looked
deeply traumatised; he had been severely interrogated at
work. A fellow elder had been shot by the Securitate a
few months ago. How long would it take him and countless
others in Romania to recover from the shock and anguish
of past years?

In the days following this first sign of overt resistance,
the vast demonstrations which took place in Timisoara
had a strong religious element. Crowds would gather
before the Orthodox cathedral in the great square of
Timisoara and on one day at least, a crowd of 120,000
people gathered, knelt down and shouted, 'There *is* a
God! There *is* a God!'

Amongst all the candles burning for the dead in
Timisoara (seven to ten thousand were estimated to
have been killed in the uprising) John saw men hacking
at the frozen ground with pickaxes. In the centre of the
square they were constructing a great wooden cross.

With Ceauşescu and his wife executed and the Securitate
conquered, even unbelievers were talking openly, saying,
'God has done this. We could never have overthrown this
regime.' Respect for the churches was obvious because
these included people who were known to have suffered much before the revolution yet were now making
every effort to help others through the post-revolutionary
confusion.

There was a spiritual harvest to be gathered in. Almost
everyone seemed open to the Gospel. Even policemen
had wept to receive Bibles. They were spiritually parched,
thirsty for the good news of Jesus Christ.

In this new climate of openness there was also an
opportunity to cross ancient barriers of mistrust between
the Romanians and the ethnic Hungarians of Transylvania.
In fact the Reformed Church itself, which had provided
the essential backdrop to the revolution, was ethnically
Hungarian. And in January 1991 the flag draping the spot
where Pastor Laszlo Tokes was arrested did not display

the red, blue and yellow of Romania but the red, white and green of Hungary.

Now both sides knew that Hungarian and Romanian blood had been shed together in freeing their country. An encouraging sign was the distribution of relief by the Reformed Church to all bereaved families after the riots in Tirgu Mures.

John's friends in the Reformed churches were aware of the need to cross the barriers, to swallow their own prejudice and go out with the Gospel of Jesus which could heal the divisions and bring peace to both ethnic groups.

John had clearly been challenged by the lives of the people he met. He spoke urgently of their needs; many Christians were traumatised by their experiences at the hands of the Securitate. Others were emotionally destroyed by the shocking events of recent weeks in which many had lost relatives.

It had been a joy to be able to bring greetings and gifts to these shaken pastors and assure them that churches in London and Scotland were praying for them. Their grateful responses, the joy in their eyes, had been reward enough for John's team.

As a pastor, of course, John focused on the needs of fellow pastors struggling to lead their liberated but bewildered flocks. The Hungarian Reformed Church in Transylvania had about 1,400 congregations who were almost entirely within the Hungarian-speaking minority of the country.

Listening to John's account, I wondered how the churches could be in any state to provide care and counsel for their members, let alone new Christians. It was a miracle that so many had survived all these years, for apart from the routine persecution, the state ensured that their living conditions were often appalling. Even if the threat to life had diminished, it was hard to foresee an immediate improvement in their daily hardship.

John told us about Leventi, a young Reformed Church assistant pastor in his late twenties ministering in Tirgu

Mures, a town in central Transylvania. His young people's group had become so popular that the authorities banished him to a remote village. Now he, his wife, a toddler and new baby were living in a little two-roomed house with no running water, no bathroom and no inside toilet. At minus twenty-six degrees, the weather only added to the deprivation. A thermometer was kept permanently in the baby's cot in case the temperature dropped too low to support life.

Three days after his wife's return from hospital with their new baby, the Securitate had arrested him. By then the revolution had begun in Timisoara and the whole country was tense; he was certain he would not see his wife and children again.

As the police car took him over the bumpy roads, he felt only shame and prayed: 'My Christian life is not what it should be; I have not been walking with my Saviour as I should have done. I will be ashamed to go and meet Him today in this spiritual condition.'

Happily the Securitate were occupied with more pressing matters and he was released to a joyous reunion with his wife late that night.

Another young pastor, Peter, had had the joy of seeing his three children share their first orange from a relief package. As they went to bed that night, they asked their mother for another.

'You'd better pray to God if you want another orange,' she advised them.

Two days later John and his friends arrived to visit them. Searching for a gift, one of the team selected a bag of oranges from the team's own food box and took it indoors to the family.

At the time he visited this family in January their entire village had been without electricity since November; a power shortage meant it was unlikely to be reconnected before March. In addition, their house was falling down. Located by a river bank, it had water seeping through the kitchen floor and mice-infested walls.

'What sort of ministry can these men have? What sort of life can they live? What needs do they have?' asked John.

Their needs seemed all too obvious and overwhelming. What could we do in the face of such continual suffering? For many, persecution had lasted for years.

These were no naïve young men. From their youth they knew the cost of being a Christian. Fully aware of the hardships involved, they had taken up their cross and followed Christ.

Now that freedom of religion had emerged after decades of suppression, there was a tremendous need for truth. With the reawakening of the nation's spiritual curiosity came the potential for thousands of conversions, John believed. People had said to him, 'The revolution has given our country a new head, but our country needs a new heart also – and only God can give us a new heart.'

Most of all there was a need for younger men in the ministry like Leventi and Peter to take a lead in evangelism by reaching out to their fellow countrymen with the good news of Jesus Christ. With the state Church under the control of the Ministry of Cults and Religions, older men in the Church like the bishops had been obliged to work with the Securitate and were now seen as compromised quislings.

John said we should thank God for these young men's faithfulness and pray for every effort to advance the cause of Christ.

His visit had also been intensely practical. As well as medical supplies their minibus had carried many bags of food, clothes, shoes and hot-water bottles which they distributed to pastors in Tirgu Mures, Brasov, Fagaras and Oradea. They were encouraged to see many lorries carrying food from Holland, yet realised that the need was only just beginning to be met.

'It's rather pathetic,' John admitted, 'that you feel satisfied to see a great mountain of supplies in a pastor's house or church hall being sorted by women from the congregation. But by the time they have divided it between 250 families, each home gets one small box containing one packet each of salt and sugar, a tub of margarine, and two or three tins. I don't know how many boxes you bring home from your weekly visit to the supermarket, but one box like that for a family with four or five children wouldn't last very long.'

Then he finished with a memorable request.

'Pray,' he said, 'that God would change *your* heart and *your* life and make you a lively servant of his.'

I knew I had never felt so compelled to get up and do something. Somehow I *had* to be involved with these people. So often we feel concerned by suffering we see on television or read about in the newspapers. But then the phone rings and our daily concerns take over. We go and put the kettle on – and almost before there has been time to pray about it, that particular situation has been left far behind.

This time the plight of the Romanian Christians remained with me; I could not relinquish these images even if I had wanted to do so. John and his family came to visit me in Lolworth showing the slides which had illustrated his talks. Formerly suspicious policemen posed proudly with Bibles, tearful middle-aged women clutched at New Testaments, haggard ministers and their families lined up next to piles of donated food, trying to smile their gratitude.

Suddenly it dawned on me that in all the rush by Western Christians to get help into Romania, it was a sad fact that the women were being left out. Our team, like others, had mainly met ministers, restricting their contacts to the men. But who was seeing what the women needed? It was the women who had to bring up the children and run households in what we would call primitive conditions, often combining an outside job to make ends meet. My heart went out to them; I so wanted to talk to these women and find out what help they wanted.

And it was not only the women who needed practical help. Along with the rest of the world I was appalled to

learn of Romania's orphans. Almost daily I saw pictures
of Ceauşescu's orphanages. His solution to the population
problem of his own making was to store unwanted children
in buildings little better than human warehouses.

'Orphan' was an ironic term in itself; too often the
listless brown eyes belonged to a child who was born
into a family which did not want and could not support
him. Perhaps abandoned at the roadside, they were kept
in rows of cots, fifty at a time, which lined bare walls. No
one knew the age of any child and no one could have asked
the child itself – few of them had been stimulated to talk
at an early age. Baths and medical care (many children
were thought to have AIDS) were as rare as attention,
lights and heating were low and sanitation unspeakable.

Yet though much moved, I knew that there was really
nothing I could do personally apart from pray.

Then one night, sitting with my little dog Topsy on my
knee, I found myself crying as I watched yet another report
on Romanian orphanages. Topsy sensed my sorrow and
snuggled closer. She always demanded cuddles because
she herself had been an ill-treated orphan. When I rescued
her, the thin, hairless body was covered in cigarette burns.
Now she was happy and healthy, but who would cuddle
and tease those thousands of unloved children rocking
mindlessly in their cots all day, peering between the bars
at strange cameramen as they provided a few shocking
minutes of viewing in comfortable, centrally heated First
World homes?

A verse from Mark's Gospel flashed into my mind:
'Suffer the little children to come unto me, and forbid
them not: for of such is the Kingdom of God.' (Mark
10: 14, AV)

All at once a sense of my inconsistency overwhelmed
me. Was I, a totally committed Christian, really meant to
spend my retirement cherishing a pet and doing very little
for humans with real needs?

Still I was uncertain as to whether the ideas coming to
me now were part of God's plan for me. Over the years

I had learned never to make major changes impulsively;
I always waited for the backing of Scripture.

There was not a long wait. One of the apostle Paul's
visions in Acts 16: 6–10 made a tremendous impact on
me during one of my daily Bible readings. I digested it
and recommitted my new ideas to God in my prayers. A
few days later I was watching another report on Romania
when the same words cut across my thoughts: 'Come over
to help us' (v. 9).

Paul had been called to Macedonia two thousand years
ago. In his vision, a man from Macedonia stood and
begged him to come and help them.

I knew I had heard from God in the way He had always
communicated with me. The first thing I did was to make
an appointment to see my GP, Dr Golden. Her reply to
my questions was what I had hoped.

'Nothing worthwhile is ever easy. Pain you have now
would be the same in Romania as in Harrow.'

I was satisfied.

By May 1990 there was no doubt left in my mind. After
our Sunday morning service I went up to John Nicholls.
What I said next was more of an announcement than a
request: 'I want to go to Romania.'

2

Here Am I, Send Me

So many people thought it was wrong for me to go to Romania. I had real opposition, yet as events were to prove, God had specific work for me there.

I knew that 'With God all things are possible' (Matthew 19:26, NKJV) and the fact that I was past my sell-by date, according to this world's standards, was irrelevant. I was absolutely sure that I had a 'calling' to the people of Romania.

Jesus said, 'Take up your cross and follow me' (Matthew 16:24). A cross was made from a rough tree and carrying that on your shoulder would hurt. My right shoulder has been very badly injured and is always a problem. To put a rough tree trunk on that shoulder would be excruciatingly painful; if it was on the other one I would simply fall over. The cross for Jesus was dereliction and an excruciating death (and of course the conquering of death), so why should we expect our Christian service to be without pain or effort?

I could honestly not understand why so many people thought I should stay at home simply because the way ahead would be difficult for me.

However, none of us anticipated the mountain paths where I would be led. The climb up can take every ounce of strength you have, but the air is so much purer and sweeter the higher you climb – and without seeing it, who can imagine the beauty and majesty of the view from the mountain top?

Now when I first told John Nicholls, my minister, about

my desire to go to Romania, his first reaction was a sharp intake of breath.

'Are you sure?' he asked. 'Be sure to take out a medical insurance.'

He was, of course, genuinely concerned for my health because of my need of a stick, and the fact that a serious road accident in 1980 had left me with other disabilities and fairly persistent pain. Eleven years earlier I had had major back surgery.

Dr Golden had already greatly encouraged me when she pointed out that pain is the same wherever one goes! She ensured I would have enough pain-killing medication for the journey and wished she could have done something similar herself, because she was so concerned about the Romanian situation.

I was also able to talk to one of the church elders, Iain Mcleod, who was a wise young man. 'If you really want to go,' he told me, 'there isn't really any way that we can influence you.'

Once people realised that I was going because I was sure of my call from God to go to Romania and do something to help, I did get encouragement from the many caring and informed Christians in my congregation.

One couple, Donald and Chrismina Morrison, who live close by, provided some early encouragement in a rather backhanded way! Chrismina, who always claimed to be frightened but fond of me, because I do speak my mind, said, 'If you believe that you should go, that's good enough for me.' They later laboured for hours, helping pack boxes, and are now valued friends!

But it was my friends outside church who, knowing me rather better than those in my congregation, were openly supportive from the beginning. I went to Cambridge again to see the Raynars. Like me, John felt that years should give one a little bit of wisdom, and was pleased I was using mine!

The greatest support of all came from Norman and Sally Stone (*née* Magnusson). I had known Norman, now

a television director, for many years since he came to
London as a student. Sally was a television presenter. I
first saw her on television in Scotland, heard she was a
Christian and thought, 'That's just the girl for Norman!'
After that I started praying that they might meet, which
they eventually did, to everyone's delight. They now
have four children and are the closest I have to family
in England.

I was able to tell Norman about Romania on one
occasion when he came to see me after I had been
unwell. While he was unloading the boxes of food he
had brought to stock up my freezer, I told him what was
on my heart.

'Well, you've got to get yourself well first,' he responded
cautiously. 'But if you have to go, we'll support you.'

After that their support, both in prayer and financially,
was invaluable to me. Like Dr Golden, they would have
liked to be able to go themselves, and gave probably more
than they could afford to ensure I was able to buy the drugs
I needed to take to Romanian families.

Sally also gave me lots of children's clothes, and an
adult's new Icelandic cardigan which I knew she loved
herself. Her reasoning was, 'Why shouldn't they have
something beautiful?'

Some people give things to charity which should really
be thrown out, like rusty tins of food, but Norman and
Sally, along with others, gave of their best. Meanwhile,
I made my own enquiries about the items the Romanian
women would like to maintain their daily lives. It was the
450th anniversary of the Reformed Church in Hungary,
and the area I hoped to visit, Tirgu Mures in Transylvania,
used to belong to Hungary. The Free Church of Scotland
sent the Chairman of its Foreign Missions Board to
represent it at the Church's celebrations in June 1990. As
I knew him, I phoned him and asked him to find out what
would be useful for me to take. I was certain that items like
needles, thread and knitting wool would be most useful,
because the Romanians were enthusiastic needlewomen.

There was also an orphanage at Tirgu Mures which had great medical needs. First aid equipment would be useful, too, as there were almost no medical supplies in the country; it would be helpful to have a basic stock in each manse.

In response to these messages, I received a letter from Tirgu Mures asking for all the items on my list and assuring me of a welcome if I could make the journey. They would also have liked much more medical equipment, costing hundreds of thousands of pounds, but I knew this was not part of my job at that stage, although the work to establish a medical centre was to take over my life later.

My job for the time being was to make families' lives a little easier, which meant taking basic medical equipment. Here again Dr Golden was so helpful. She spent a considerable time sorting out lists of drugs for me to take over.

Making contacts was no problem. There were people whom John knew and others I had heard of over a number of years whom I was longing to meet. I simply needed to get in touch with them in order to go out and encourage them. In the end, they encouraged me!

From March onwards my house had been filling up with secondhand clothes and other practical items people had thought might be useful for Romanian families. The girls working at my doctor's surgery started collecting clothes and Sally contacted lots of her friends, but even so a great deal of clothes arrived from people I had never met; it was astonishing.

I wanted to take lots of first aid equipment, while Dr Golden insisted we remembered the expectant mothers. We gathered together loads of vitamins and iron for the mothers, which turned out to be even more welcome than I had imagined. In the end I had £3,000 worth of medical supplies, mostly paid for by Norman and Sally and an old friend working in Saudi Arabia. As well as the two big donations, there were many donations of £10 and £20 from my friends around the country. I also contributed from my own savings, which I wanted to do. My chemist was tremendously helpful: as well as lots of advice, he helped me apply for VAT exemption, which saved a substantial sum.

Children's clothes were sent to me from all over the country. Many had to be mended and washed. Sometimes there were children's clothes on the line three times a day! But I couldn't have taken anything dirty or torn to Romania; they had enough problems already.

Sally helped me sort the children's clothes, while Donald and Chrismina helped pack. Of all the preparations, it was the packing which took the longest.

For months I was working until two or three a.m. As soon as I got one lot boxed up, more bags of clothes would arrive. My big spare room and the dining-room were filled with boxes; often I would be in my sitting-room, with nowhere to sit, surrounded by piles of clothes sorted into age groups.

And then at the last moment the medical equipment from my chemist came; packing all this was another job in itself.

I planned to fly over, but also tried hard to get a driver and vehicle for the other end, because I have to drive an adapted car and could not travel long distances alone.

I am afraid nobody wanted to go with me. At times I got desperate and would pray about it, but the conviction I should go never wavered. That conviction had crystallised when I heard John's tape. My decision to go was not born out of feelings of compassion, although I had certainly felt a partner in these people's sorrows. But if mere feelings had produced my desire to go, they would have evaporated in the face of all the discouragement. It was, it seemed, God who wanted me to go. All the Scriptures I read confirmed that I should go; and those verses from Acts 16: 6–10 kept coming back to me: 'Come over to help us.'

I knew I had the concern and, I believed, the mental and emotional energy to assess what was needed there and get something done. And having received confirmation through Scripture, no one else's opinion really came into it.

Although I knew I was doing what God wanted, it was tempting to feel lonely at this time. And two particular events were to emphasise my aloneness in the whole venture.

During all the preparations, Topsy became more and more distressed. The piles of boxes meant she no longer had the run of the house and she was used to being able to play where she pleased.

On 8th September 1990, she asked to be let out at midnight. This was unusual, but perhaps she was feeling the lack of space.

I had never let her out on her own, but was working against the clock, trying to get some space cleared in my sitting-room ready for Sunday. Each Saturday I cleaned the house and made sure there was food ready for the next day, in case a stranger at church needed a welcoming home. I let her out knowing her to be a sensible little dog. She must have seen a cat and run into the road. Five minutes later she was dead – hit by a car.

The people over the road picked her up and took her to their home. I was out calling her when they phoned. I went over to see them; they were very kind but would not let me take Topsy home, which was probably for the best as I was in a state of shock. I was back there at 8.45 a.m. the next morning:

'Please can I take Topsy home,' I asked.

Back at home I laid her on her favourite bean bag. I phoned Donald Morrison, whom I was due to take to church: 'I can't come to church. Topsy's been killed and I don't know where to bury her.' My previous dog, Sabra, had been buried in Lolworth but this would be impractical.

Donald agreed that another couple, Iain and Alison, in whose garden I had been doing a lot of work, might allow Topsy to be buried there.

I phoned Iain to ask him about Topsy: 'Donald's already phoned me,' he replied. 'Of course you can.'

He and Alison were going out to lunch after church, but cancelled it so Topsy could be buried that afternoon. Donald had decided to come and collect me for church, so I left Topsy behind on her bean bag wrapped in a white sheet.

Everyone at church was most concerned about Topsy. They all loved her because she came with me nearly every Sunday and sat in a basket under my pew. As long as she had a choc drop for the sermon she never moved until it was all over.

That Sunday one dear young man came over to ask if I was unwell.

'Topsy was killed this morning,' I explained between sniffs.

He started to weep as well.

After church we buried my dear Topsy in the garden where she had played.

For those with a family, the death of a pet can be grievous enough. But for those like myself, who have to rely on friends and church 'family' for support, a pet is the only being 'on the spot' in one's daily life. I had some cousins left in Scotland, but my immediate family was in Australia and New Zealand.

In addition, Topsy and I had a special relationship ever since I had rescued her from gipsies who were ill-treating her. They had threatened to 'come and get me' after I had taken Topsy to the RSPCA, but I challenged them with the fact that the police would want to know where Topsy, whose hair had been burned away, had got her fourteen cigarette burns and an injury to her back leg. I was careful not to go straight home after that, but they never came. Topsy had every worm you could think of, colonies of fleas and no inkling about house-training, having lived in damp grass under a caravan.

It took seven months of 'quarantine' in my kitchen and lavatory before Topsy was house-trained and could sleep on my bed at night with my other dog, Sabra, another rescued stray. Once Topsy was trained, she remained the cleanest, dearest dog one could imagine, even though she tried to usurp Sabra's place as top dog. She was able to succeed to this status when poor Sabra died at the age of sixteen and a half.

Topsy was a bit of a scatterbrain, but she lived to please me and I had loved her as my own child. The fact that she had been killed because I was too busy to go out with her meant I spent quite some time reproaching myself.

But while I was mourning Topsy I also had to continue collecting supplies. It was the only sensible thing to do. Then came another blow.

Since John Nicholls had made his trip to Romania with a group from Scotland experienced in such journeys, it seemed correct to link up with them to arrange my own journey. During many, many telephone calls to Scotland, I was encouraged each time, but we never seemed to be making any concrete progress. This was strange, because at my end I already had addresses of Romanians to see, and up-to-date information about things they needed.

I knew I was working on the right lines, and was surprised at the lack of support from that particular group. To be fair, they did offer me a minibus with the promise of drivers, but no drivers ever materialised! By September I was ready to go, but had to keep postponing my departure date while I waited for definite information from Scotland.

Around the same time I was told of an American who wanted to go, so I put him in touch with Scotland. Then one morning, just four days after Topsy's death, the phone rang at seven fifteen a.m. It was the American, who spent three-quarters of an hour on the phone from California reporting to me the conversation he had had with my Scottish contact, and pleading with me not to go.

What he had heard about me was most uncompli-mentary and very hurtful. I still don't understand why one person, Christian or not, deliberately seeks to hurt

another. All I could repeat to the American was the fact
that I had received a most enthusiastic invitation from
Romania. He, dear man, was surprised to learn this.

When I put the phone down, I was shaking all over. I
was in a rather low state after Topsy's death, and burst
into tears when I spoke to my minister the next Sunday.

John immediately advised me to go ahead on my own.
Just back from a preaching visit to Romania himself, he
encouraged me to stick to my original plan. I would fly
with British Airways, who had already agreed to transport
the medical equipment free of charge. In Budapest I
had friends, the Magays. I phoned the husband, Tamas,
who offered to speak to the Hungarian–Maltese Charity
Service. At first they said they would meet me at the
airport with a van and driver, only to withdraw and then
extend the invitation again. It changed several times, but
eventually the arrangement seemed to be settled.

It still seemed as if I was going on my own until the
end of September when my friend Helen Gray, who
had been very concerned about my going, agreed to
accompany me.

It was sad that I ended up making all my own arrangements, because the Scottish group had been very successful
at getting Bibles behind the Iron Curtain when Eastern
Europe was closed, but God moves on and others like
myself were being prompted by the Holy Spirit to play
our parts in helping the East Europeans. God used this
discouragement to benefit me, because from then on
John gave me all the support possible, although probably
holding some reservations about my physical strength. He
knew of the amount of work I had already done, which
proved I was not leaning on others to carry out my call.

Equally reassuring was the remark of one of the elders'
wives. After I had spoken with John, she came up to me
and said, 'Helen, you put us all to shame. I wish more of
us could do what you're doing.'

Looking back, however, I can be grateful for some of the
opposition, because it made me depend more completely

on God; it was only from Him that I would receive help and strength.

I had been told it was not God's will for me to go to Romania and my character had been questioned, but I hope whoever reads these pages can profit from what I learnt. If you are sure God wants you to do something, please take it to Him in prayer, read the Bible, and seek His confirmation. When you're sure, with absolute conviction, that God is guiding you in a certain direction and you have peace in your heart about it, don't let others put you off.

The determination to obey God's call had, I believe, something to do with my early life. My early years, spent in New Zealand, had given me a great independence.

Our farm ran to thousands of acres, much of it bush with great rocks on tops of ridges. I knew every tree in the bush, every bird nest and where the trout lived under the river banks. My great longing was to be a singer and out in the bush I would practise singing, seeing how many echoes I could get. I would try to imitate the tui, a bird with a wonderfully rich, rounded tone. If I hadn't tried to do that, I don't believe my voice would have developed as it did.

Riding ten miles to school every morning helped make me self-reliant. In winter I took a chisel to dislodge frozen snow from the frog inside the horse's shoes. Once at the one-roomed school, the teacher had red-hot pokers ready in the coal-and-wood fire to melt the snow. The horses spent the rest of the day in a five-acre paddock outside until we were ready to saddle up again and ride home. It's no wonder I love animals now; I lived for my horses in those days, which was a good thing, as I had to be up very early to groom and feed them before setting off.

My spiritual education was just as thorough as my practical one. I was brought up with a chapter of the Bible and a chapter of Scottish history each day. My mother had a living faith, which my father did not share; he became bitter after suffering dreadful injuries in the First World

War, so my mother kept quiet about her relationship with the Lord, although her example spoke volumes. Even so, a Scottish education had ensured my father knew the Bible backwards, and could always quote contradictory chapter and verse to any Jehovah's Witnesses!

We were not allowed to go to church, and in any case lived too far away from one, but my father would read us a chapter of the Bible at night.

These were the influences which shaped the way I think and react. I can't cross the road when I see someone in trouble; not only would I deny the master I follow, but I would be denying what my mother had taught me, and the early memories of my grandmother.

Things were not always idyllic. I remember an occasion when my father and I had been out mustering and were bringing about eight hundred sheep down to the sheepyards. Suddenly my father fell from his horse. My mother appeared as I was dismounting. I knelt down and cried out to God to deliver us and help my father. In later years, when I was rebellious and trying to live my own life, not considering it belonged to God, my mother often reminded me of that occasion when I had cried out to God for His help.

Boarding school followed my free and easy country school; it was a shock to the system as I was more used to the rugby ball than the basket ball! As I was finishing school, war broke out in 1939. My brother went off to the front and later I began nursing and in 1942 I joined the Air Force. I nursed after the war as well. I didn't much enjoy it, but it was character forming. In New Zealand we were self-sufficient regarding food; we raised our own cattle and sheep for meat, milk and butter and grew our own vegetables and fruit. Naturally my mother sent food parcels to my brother and our family in Scotland. There was always the idea of sharing with those in need; it was our responsibility, not someone else's.

After the war I left home and went to live with cousins in the Wairarapa, where I continued nursing, travelling down to Wellington for weekly singing lessons with Sister Mary at the convent there. She had studied with Sister Leo in Auckland, who taught Kiri Te Kanawa many years later.

Although people thought I was so self-assured at the various performances I was asked to give, I never got over stage fright. On one occasion I was singing at a performance where the Prime Minister of New Zealand was present. Although I knew him, I was so frightened when people started applauding at the end, I gathered up my long skirt and shot down through the audience and out of the door! Nobody I know has been idiotic enough to do that!

One particular period from my past helped give me a special concern for the Romanian orphanages when I heard about them early in 1990. Part of the reason why they touched a tender chord in my heart lay in the fact that I had spent two years caring for forty-two orphaned boys in the 1940s.

It came about when I was preparing to study at the Royal Academy in London, at Sister Mary's suggestion. Wanting to be independent and not accept any money from home, I arranged to do some mending and babysitting in exchange for a room and board at the Presbyterian Social Services Orphanage in Wellington, New Zealand, which catered for forty-two boys from eighteen months to fifteen years old. The idea was that I would have plenty of time to continue my music studies.

I came home one night to find Mr Cross, the secretary of the Presbyterian Social Services Association, in the home. The matron and housemaster had walked out, leaving only me, in my early twenties, to look after the children. Thanks to the way I had been brought up, it did not occur to me to refuse. I was also fond of the boys and they got on well with me.

So I gave up the thought of the Royal Academy and became matron to forty-two boys. I moved into the flat occupied formerly by a married couple and brought the youngest boy's cot into my bedroom so I could hear if he cried in the night.

My singing did not lapse entirely; I continued lessons when possible with Sister Mary.

In the orphanage, I found myself repeating my father's tradition of the Bible at bedtime. After their showers, both big boys and little boys would come into the sitting-room, which was quite a break with tradition; they had been rather regimented until then. In they trooped, and we would have our Bible story followed by a discussion.

It was strange, as I had no living faith at that time, but we did have a very happy family life. I had to relieve the cook for a day and an afternoon each week, which meant coping with recipes requiring ingredients like ten pounds of flour. I was grateful for my mother's instruction in basic cooking! On the cooking days I was always rather stressed, because lunch had to be on the table when the boys came home from school for their midday break of just one hour.

It wasn't easy, but it was very rewarding. I still look back at that time with a great sense of accomplishment, not just about the housekeeping side, but about my relationship with the boys. Even after I went to Italy to pursue my singing career, some of them wrote to me for several years and I kept their photos. I kept in touch with one, Colin Smith, until I went to London, but lost the connection because I was too busy to answer his letters, so if he reads this book, I do apologise!

In fact I was so fond of two brothers that I applied to adopt them, but as a single woman was not eligible. It was just as well, in the light of my subsequent experiences!

The next stage of my career began when the Italian government gave me a scholarship to further my singing studies in Italy. I was captivated by Italy and seriously considered taking Italian citizenship. I never had a great career, but I really loved performing, although it had me in a constant state of terror! Verdi's mezzo ladies were my forte; I found it easy to get inside the roles and they particularly suited my voice.

It was in Italy that I met Dr Francis Schaeffer who later became well-known through L'Abri Fellowship. I went to stay with him and his wife in Switzerland and on a mountain walk he asked, 'Helen, are you a Christian?'

I quickly replied, 'Of course, I was born in a Christian country.'

Later, as I listened to many conversations in their warm, hospitable chalet, I found that the deep questions which I had never been honest enough to ask were being answered.

Every answer would be prefixed, 'The Bible says,' and I had much food for thought. We went for another mountain walk and again I was asked if I was a Christian. This time my reply was different. I meekly replied, 'I don't know.' Francis Schaeffer said he didn't know either, but suggested I go into my room, read my Bible and pray.

I didn't know where to start, but as I lived in Rome, I started in the book of Romans. The first chapter condemned me; by the time I got to the sixth chapter I felt there was no hope for me; then came that wonderful opening verse of chapter 8: 'Therefore, there is now no condemnation for those who are in Christ Jesus . . .'

I fell to my knees and prayed the first believing, God-honouring prayer of my life and there, high up in the Swiss Alps, a mountain rolled off my back. I was forgiven and reconciled with God my maker!

To say my life was turned upside-down is no exaggeration. All my personal relationships had to be thought out more carefully, my career re-examined and indeed my whole future.

For a start, I had been thinking of getting married, but that was not to be because my fiancé did not share my love of God.

My calling was also now open to God's loving scrutiny. Suddenly I knew that I no longer wanted to remain in the theatre; I preferred to work with people. It was when auditioning at Covent Garden, that I became convinced of this. I ran out of the theatre, and went back to stay with my cousin George in Scotland. While there I developed some health problems and, very much like my father in his firmness, George persuaded me that returning to Italy was unwise. For some years I stayed in Glasgow, sharing a house with a friend.

When I eventually moved down to London in 1970, it was to work with the International Jewish Society, now known as Christian Witness to Israel. I have a great love for the Jews, because my every blessing has come through these people. When I had to take early retirement from Christian Witness to Israel, due to my road accident, it was a very sad day.

This was the first time I had felt a major call to certain work. It was to be echoed years later in the call to Romania. One or two of my Jewish contacts, with whom I continually discuss their Messiah, also gave me support and encouragement to go to Romania.

Already a member of the Free Church of Scotland for many years, I transferred to our London congregation now at Cole Abbey Church near St Paul's Cathedral. With the arrival of John Nicholls as our minister, many have been added to the church. Our membership is from many different parts of the world and as a fellowship we do experience the rich blessings of God. We owe much to John Nicholls. The congregation is mostly young, but all age groups are represented, from new babes to one dear lady in her nineties. Going to church was a major part of my week; that and visiting Norman and Sally, writing to my relatives and caring for my dogs.

For many years I had been privileged to work with and for other people; now, in my late sixties, I assumed that I had been through enough adventures in my life and it seemed perfectly fitting to slow down! I honestly believed that the Romania trip would be a single visit, simply to take supplies and offer some encouragement to the women.

Several of my congregation were still worried about my going, but I think they thought I was far more frail than I am. I do get dreadfully tired, but I'm still able to do quite a lot and there's no way anyone will be able to pack me up in cotton wool. I'd rather wear out than rust out!

However, if I had known what lay ahead, I think I might have wavered . . . But I didn't, so I went ahead in faith and hope, unaware that in a year's time I would have incontrovertible proof that it had been right for me to go to Romania; and one little boy would be alive because of it.

3

Topsy's Children

Before Topsy died, I had told her that I was going away, but that I would come back with many children for her to play with. As the funds came in to support my initial trip, I opened a building society account, under the name of 'Topsy's Children'. After Topsy was killed, I felt this name, jokingly applied at first, was now far too important to change and when we became a registered charity in April 1991, it was as Topsy's Children's Trust.

I had bought all the drugs I could, as I believed the Hungarian–Maltese charity was supplying the minibus. It had been a lot of hard work almost entirely on my own, and although others had been helpful when time permitted, it was my life and home that had been turned upside-down! I had listed all the medical supplies which filled seventeen boxes and two suitcases. With my own suitcase as well, there was no room on that trip for all the clothes I had been given.

However, all the other arrangements seemed to have fallen into place. Contact with Romania by phone at that time simply did not exist. So even though it was known that we were coming, nobody knew when.

John was relieved that Helen Gray was to accompany me; although I had been prepared to go on my own, I knew my church would be happier if I had a companion. I was also very grateful because one of my Scottish friends, a minister, had said, 'I would definitely take it as the Lord's instruction that you are not to go if there is no one able to go with you.'

I had known Helen, a fairly recent Christian, for six years. She was always bright and cheerful, which I was to appreciate greatly. Helen's husband had finally agreed to her coming, and Helen had managed to get time off work in order to travel with me. I had booked us into an hotel in Tirgu Mures through a Romanian travel agent based in London, paying for it in advance to ensure that we would not be a burden to anyone in Romania. I also had several contacts, whom John Nicholls had suggested, and had arranged to go to one of their homes on arrival in Tirgu Mures. Now we were all set to leave on 15th October 1990.

On 12th October, three days before we were due to leave, my friend Tamas phoned from Hungary.

'I'm very sorry,' he began, but the Maltese charity has a big party coming from Germany and there will be no vehicles available. What will I do?'

'Can you hire a vehicle for us?' I asked. I knew this could only be done in Budapest; British companies refused to hire out vehicles for Romania at that time due to the high rate of theft. It was for the same reasons of security that airlines would not fly into Romania; hence our roundabout route via Budapest.

Endless phone calls to Budapest followed – I had enormous bills! The number of times our plans changed was incredible.

Finally Tamas had good news from Hertz in Budapest; they would hire out a minibus to us for two days. The charity could still let us have one of their drivers who would bring the vehicle back to Budapest as soon as we had unloaded, in order to keep costs down. We would return from Romania under our own steam.

Unbelievably, I finally got to the airport at 7.15 a.m. on 15th October. A kind friend, Pauline Timson, brought her car full of boxes and Donald drove my adapted car, also full. An incredulous porter helped us take my two carloads of boxes into the terminal. Helen brought two more boxes, so it really was too much to expect British Airways to take it all free. Happily I only had to pay £130 excess and Helen paid about £16.

Arriving at Budapest Airport brought the joy of seeing my friend Tamas waiting for us. A lexicographer, he had stayed with me while compiling a Hungarian–English dictionary for Collins. His wife Kati and their daughters had also stayed with me at different times; I really felt part of their family, particularly when I received photos of each new grandchild.

Tamas helped us clear Customs, then completed the formalities for the minibus with Hertz and introduced us to our driver, András Solti, a young man of about twenty, who helped get the van loaded up. I don't know how I would have managed without the help of Tamas. How good it is to have old friends willing to put themselves out for you!

While András was taking the minibus to his charity's warehouse, Tamas took Helen and me to his home, where we rested until Kati arrived home from work (she taught at a college). It was not a typical East European block of flats, because Hungary is far from being a Third World country. Tamas and Kati owned a small but artistically decorated flat in a lovely, clean building with welcoming plants in the entrance hall. In fact, it was only the toilet paper which betrayed the fact that the consumer did not have a choice!

Kati made us a meal and at ten p.m. András came to pick us up in the loaded minibus.

On the way to the Hungarian–Romanian border, our minibus, which was, we understood, only six months old, began to cough and splutter. András could not find anything significantly wrong under the bonnet, but it meant we only progressed at a snail's pace. With all the confidence of a very young man he did not seem to take the vehicle's misbehaviour very seriously; from his almost non-existent English I gathered that he was quite certain we would reach Tirgu Mures in that bus.

I countered my fears that we could later break down in

the lonely Carpathian Mountains, miles from anywhere, with the thought, 'If God's brought us this far, He is surely going to see us safely to our destination.'

There was enough room in the van for us each to have a spacious seat, but I could not rest for all the jerking from the engine. Helen managed to sleep through it but I lay awake contemplating what had brought me to this point and wondering what lay ahead.

Whom have I in heaven but You?
And there is none upon earth that I desire besides You.
My flesh and my heart fail;
But God is the strength of my heart and my portion
    forever. (Psalm 73: 25–6, NKJV)

Jerking along, we eventually reached the Hungarian–Romanian border at one a.m. We filled in all the forms required, and I thanked the Lord for the trouble I had taken in compiling my lists of medical supplies. They proved to be most useful for convincing border guards of their contents! The Hungarians started to unload the van, but when they saw I had everything listed, they just said, 'Go.'

At one of our many stops for András to stretch his legs, he suddenly tapped on the window, gesturing to me to come out. He wanted me to survey the sky above. Not since my New Zealand childhood had I seen such a glorious, black velvet sky, with stars high above sparkling like diamonds. The Carpathian mountains were spectacularly beautiful in the starlight.

The heavens declare the glory of God;
the skies proclaim the work of his hands.
Day after day they pour forth speech;
night after night they display knowledge.
There is no speech or language
where their voice is not heard.

Their voice goes out into all the earth,
their words to the ends of the world.
(Psalm 19:1–4, NIV)

'Can you doubt that this is the work of God?' I asked
him. I was not sure if his shrug was one of unbelief or
uncomprehension . . . Proof that we were now in Romania
was provided by the pitiful figures walking along in the
pre-dawn gloom. All in black, many were bent and I could
not have said if they were actually elderly or not; certainly
one would not find such sights in Hungary. I was just glad
I had some things which might make some of their lives a
little easier.

There were horses and carts trailing along the roadside
as in Hungary, but here the carts were only about three
foot wide and many of the horses were thin and lame. I
would have liked to gather them all up and nurse them
back to health! There were also oxen pulling hay carts;
they seemed better cared for than the horses. It was as
though I was travelling back to a Byzantine age.

As the daylight came, we saw lots of geese, ducks,
sheep and goats on the road. I had not slept for a good
twenty-four hours, but I marvelled at the beauty of the
mountains and countryside, some of the few areas of life
the Communists had not been able to despoil.

We arrived in Tirgu Mures at about nine fifteen a.m.
Romanian time, which being October was just one hour
ahead of British time; for the rest of the year the difference
is two hours.

We went straight to the manse of Dénes Fulop and his
wife Ileana, one of the couples I had contacted; they knew
we were coming, but not the precise date.

The Romanians go in for gates and walls in a big way,
which is surely symbolic of their search for private identity
in an intrusive state. The manse was no exception; massive
wooden gates were set into the front of their house;
nothing is set back from the street, and buildings rise up
on either side of footpaths. Theirs was an old house, very

solid but looking more like an institution than a private home with bars covering the windows as it was near the town centre.

We rang the bell and Ileana, our hostess, came to the door in her dressing-gown, smiling but limping slightly with a bandaged ankle. She was in her late forties, and such a warm lady. It was a good thing she was so welcoming, because their church was now the recipient of many aid convoys from the West. Later she told us, 'Before the revolution, I had such a quiet life – I never saw anybody. Now I can't make a cup of coffee without someone from Holland or Germany or Britain coming to the door with things.'

The warmth of the welcome we received swept away the remaining fears I had brought away with me that someone of my age would not be useful in Romania. My grey hairs were no barrier whatsoever, and this encouraged me immensely. Out there they were waiting for me to arrive, showing a welcome which increased with subsequent visits. For me, such a welcome was almost embarrassing, as I was unused to being enveloped in a close family fellowship with people I did not know intimately. And that was very precious for someone on their own.

Inside the house, Ileana directed András to unload the boxes into one of the family's bedrooms – the only space available. Space was at a premium; there were a couple of other bedrooms, a study for Dénes and a small sitting-room with a bed-settee. There were very few beds; many families used bed-settees to save space. Paintings hung on most of the walls; this was one of the few things Romanians could invest in, because Ceauşescu had confiscated everything else. There was also Hungarian embroidery on every wall and Hungarian pottery. A big, tiled, gas-fired stove reached up to the ceiling.

The kitchen was basic; to make toast for breakfast Ileana had to put a bent, iron grill shelf over the gas ring. There was a large, old, stone sink, and I could see that preparing any food was labour-intensive. But although she was clearly in pain from her ankle, she insisted on making our breakfast. 'I like,' she claimed. 'I do it for God.'

As the result of a fall, her ankle was bandaged with some poor-quality non-stretch fabric, so after consulting my list I unpacked the correct box for crêpe bandages and strapped her ankle. This happened within forty-five minutes of my arrival!

She gave András some breakfast and signed his papers to prove the items were for charity. After helping us unload, András had to set off immediately to get the van back to Budapest before our rental expired.

There was no chance of our wasting any time on the trip, despite the fact I had not slept for twenty-seven hours! After discovering that the doctor could not come for her medical supplies until five p.m., Ileana walked us the four hundred yards to the town's orphanage and by ten thirty a.m. we were seeing our first group of three- to six-year-old Romanian orphans.

I have to confess that I did not take to the orphanage director, although he was very kind. He was a chainsmoker who kissed my hand with the cigarette still in his mouth!

The administrator, however, was the dearest Romanian lady, Neli Murisan, who later invited us to her home for a meal. We communicated in Italian, using gestures to fill in the gaps in our vocabulary.

When Neli took us in to see the children, there were sixteen or seventeen of them sitting at empty tables. I had no idea what they were supposed to be doing; there was certainly nothing for them play with – no books, paper or toys of any sort.

As we walked in, we were enveloped by one huge mass movement of little bodies, arms and legs flailing. Within seconds I had five children suspended from my body. Little legs and arms locked around me as they cried, 'Mama, Mama, Mama!'

I was torn between wanting to cuddle them all at once and trying to protect the rather sore places I have sustained over the years. With one child's arms round my neck, one swinging from my shoulders and one clasping my waist behind me, this was difficult. Nor did they let go for a full five minutes, during which I prayed my neck would not give out! Reason does not reach those little ones desperate for human contact. The poor wee mites finally let me go when Neli told them off in no uncertain terms.

The children didn't look very attractive. Boys and girls alike had their heads shaved regularly to protect them from lice, and they all wore little blue smocks on top of whatever clothes were available – usually trousers. Nobody had a matching pair of shoes; if a child had more than one shoe they were probably one wellington and one sandal.

They all seemed to have colds and runny noses. Helen had taken some handkerchiefs, so one of the staff took a handkerchief and wiped all their noses with it! How can you keep children healthy in those conditions?

But there were some very kind people in that orphanage, although others had no interest in the children at all. That sort of work requires a calling, and, sadly, childcare had very low status in Romania.

The room itself, which had once been whitewashed, was not too bad considering the children spent their days in it. Apart from the tables and chairs there was only a big stove in the corner, but it was smashed. The staff were at pains to point out that the 'dreadful children broke everything', but maybe if they had been stimulated to play and think they would not have behaved so badly.

We were shown the kitchen, primitive by our standards, which seemed quite clean, although it had chipped concrete floors and no one had any disinfectant to ensure hygiene was maintained.

The main room of the orphanage had obviously been the pride of the building when a private home; it had a high ceiling, carved wood and cornices. But our eyes were immediately drawn to the piles of cardboard boxes from the West filling the entire room. Apparently they were waiting to be sorted, so after playing with the children,

Helen and I willingly went to work, helped by some of the attendants.

Most of the boxes contained toys; new, old and broken toys. In fact, another aid lorry arrived from Holland while we were there and chose to drive on to another orphanage when they saw how many toys we already had. There was no doubt that Tirgu Mures, as a central town, had received more aid than other areas.

We worked on the boxes for about six hours. The toys ranged from broken pencils to little packages with a message such as 'With love from Thomas, nine years' from somewhere like Cornwall or Wales. When we had finished, there were piles of soft toys, hard toys, dolls, educational toys and books.

There were such good educational toys that I asked the helpers if I could work with each child for ten minutes using these toys. The children didn't look very bright, but that was simply a lack of stimulation. For a reason I did not discover until later, I was not granted permission.

After leaving the orphanage, we went back to the manse for our luggage and booked ourselves into our hotel, the grandly named Intercontinental. Dénes and Ileana were very cross with me for having booked a hotel, rather than letting Christians accommodate us, but it proved to be less trouble all round, even though the hotel corridors had no light bulbs and we had to grope our way along the walls at night. I had taken my own cereal for breakfast, but the hotel could not supply any milk, although all the private homes in the town had milk!

While we were waiting at the manse for the doctor to arrive, another aid crew arrived. 'A lot more people from Scotland – I don't know who they are,' announced Ileana. 'I make more food.' She was so hospitable!

I was delighted to see a group from Blythswood, a Christian aid organisation in Scotland. I didn't know any of them, but with two, Kenneth McLeod and Callum McLean, I discovered mutual friends and concerns.

Kenneth and Callum were driving out a car for a pastor

in Iasi. Graham and Frances McSween and Graham's cousin Neil were driving two forty-ton lorries packed full, also destined for Iasi. We had a great time together, and discussed the £5,000 which the Isle of Lewis had raised towards the purchase of a house to be a Christian home for children in Tirgu Mures.

I was also able to give Frances some iron tablets from my cargo because she was waiting for more to be sent from home. Having met her, I was especially shocked to learn of her death in June 1991. Frances, Graham and Neil were taking two lorries on another trip to Iasi when the McSweens' lorry went off the road. All the local people came to help, but it took six hours to free Graham from the wreckage. An ambulance plane took him back to Scotland. The ambulance carrying Frances broke down during the journey to hospital and she died on the way into the operating theatre. Frances had a real desire to help people, and they had left their two children with grandparents in order to bring aid to other families.

Soon the Christian doctor, Monika Szabo, came down to the manse with her own son Peter, who was two months old. Meeting her was like meeting an old friend; it was as if no introduction was needed. Monika was a very attractive young woman, whose total Christian commitment would make her stand out in any age or culture.

She helped me sort through all the drug boxes and showed particular interest in the vitamins and iron I had brought for expectant mothers, announcing, 'These I will take with me now.'

Monika spoke five languages, including excellent English; so many Romanians put us to shame with their language ability. I had brought two nighties and bed jackets and nice soaps for her as a personal present, knowing she had just had a baby, but she would not accept them. 'Others need them more than I do,' she insisted. John, who thought very highly of Monika, had told me she was independent, but when I pointed out that two retired ladies had sent them especially for her, she agreed to keep them. In fact, she was very thrilled when she tried them on, saying, 'I've never been so pretty.'

After Monika had left, Ileana made us all a meal and we returned to the hotel where the Blythswood contingent had also reserved rooms. We went for a walk, then returned to one of the rooms for worship. It was a most happy and blessed time of fellowship. Singing psalms, reading the Bible and praying seemed so right in the land where Ceauşescu had tried for years to block out the worship of God.

That was my first night in Romania.

4

Monika's Mothers

Next day we returned to work at the orphanage; we spent hours sorting through hundreds of boxes, and looked forward to seeing the children finally play with them.

It was not that the children were entirely neglected; on the day we left we saw the children singing and clapping their hands in a circle, led by the helpers. But the children had no love. It's all very well giving them some toys, but they've got to have a cuddle as well. The only thing those children wanted was to belong to somebody; they always called Helen and me 'Mama'. It was depressing because there was so much we wanted to do but weren't able to accomplish. I tried to give these three- to six-year-olds cuddles and hugs, and although I did not mind that they were not very clean, I became wary because all they wanted to do was rub their little noses all over me. They all had persistent colds, and my recurrent chest problems had made me rather wary of germs over the years.

Realising how little I could do for those children in the two weeks I was there was a most frustrating experience. What they needed was a permanent stand-in mother.

On my second evening in Romania Monika invited us to a prayer meeting. She stayed at home with the baby, but Laszlo, her husband, came and collected us.

It was quite an experience for me. About sixty people were present including a lot of children, who were so good one would not have known they were there. After a Bible reading, prayer commenced. Although I didn't understand Hungarian, I could tell everyone was just pouring out their hearts. I have come to know many of them since, and they were so glad to be able to meet publicly and unite with Christian brothers and sisters from far-flung places.

Coming from a church where women keep silence, I was a little uncomfortable. After forty to fifty minutes I knew beyond any shadow of doubt that everyone, and I mean *everyone*, was going to pray before that meeting finished. I didn't want to be the last and I did want to show I was part of that gathering of praying saints. There were butterflies in my tummy and I had wet, clammy hands; it was as bad as walking on stage. Why are such inhibitions inflicted on us? I was then given a calmness and a sense of aloneness with my heavenly Father and was able to approach Him as I voiced aloud my prayer.

One satisfying part of the visit was seeing the medical supplies being used. Two days later I was introduced to Marta, a lady who was expecting a baby in five weeks. She gave me a big hug and simply said, 'Thank you.' She had had three miscarriages due to severe anaemia, among other things, but I had brought the iron she desperately needed. Monika had given her the iron the night I arrived. It was touching, not only to be gratefully hugged by a stranger, but to realise that Monika, with a babe in arms, had gone all round Tirgu Mures that night giving her expectant mothers those basic nutrients that Western mothers take for granted. Now she had multi-vitamins and iron and all the other items Dr Golden had told me to take; it was hard to believe there were no iron tablets obtainable in Romania.

There was still doubt about whether the vitamins had arrived in time to save Marta's fourth baby. After I was back in England I would get up at five a.m. each day to phone Monika and learn of her progress. (It was necessary to get up early to phone because getting through to Romania was always very hard.) Marta safely gave birth to a little girl, which thrilled me. It had only been 'coincidence' that she was in Tirgu Mures visiting her parents at that time.

I worked in the orphanage for three days in all. They made Helen and me extremely welcome, even though we were not encouraged to work with the children.

Neli was delightful, and asked us to her house for a meal. She was Romanian, not Hungarian, with a charming husband and two children. Her home was more splendid than others we had seen; I assumed her husband had worked for the government before the revolution to have such luxuries as a detached house with an Alsatian guard dog and a pig in a smart sty in the garden. I like pigs, but realised that this one's days were numbered; it would be dead by mid-December in keeping with the Romanians' custom of slaughtering a whole pig for Christmas.

Like almost everyone I met, Neli was extremely hospitable; there seemed to be nothing she would not do for a guest. She was planning to turn the upper storey of her house into guest accommodation and invited me to stay there if I returned to Romania.

So how did such a warm, friendly person as Neli feel about coming back to her lovely home each evening after working in the depressing conditions of the orphanage? True, she did not work with the children, because she had an office job as administrator, but I was to remain puzzled at the contrasts in her life.

Our mutual language was Italian, which limited expression. I gathered that the orphanage was funded from Bucharest, the capital, but recently aid had been coming from the West. Donors had responded from as far away as Canada, as well as all over free Europe. It would have seemed ungrateful to pry any more.

On the fourth day, we arrived in the morning as usual and Helen went in first. She could not believe what she saw. Women were queuing up to buy bags of goods and the room where we had sorted everything was empty. Staff must have put them into the bags after we left the day before.

It appeared to us that everything was being sold off, but we had to keep silent.

The children still didn't have a pair of shoes between them, but there was nothing I could say. Any trouble-making would give them an excuse not to allow in any more people. It had been a great privilege for us to be admitted to the orphanage in the first place, because the Church had been trying to gain access for a long time but had been repeatedly put off, whereas we had been allowed in every day.

I knew Neli could not be behind it, but when I asked her what was happening, she did not appear remotely embarrassed. 'These things have to go where they are needed,' she replied.

So why was money being exchanged? Was it too much to hope that it would be used to buy other items for the orphanage? Perhaps the order came from Bucharest; after all, it was a state-run orphanage. Certainly there were signs of money being spent: the building was being painted, new washing machines installed and new wooden cots provided for the children. Their lot had been improved tremendously, but there was still a great need.

All the children slept in cots, whether they were babies or six-year-olds, and the cots were jammed together in the two dormitories. After lunch they were taken for a rest and the dormitory doors were locked. Later in the afternoon they were let out to play outside, but many were barefoot and there was broken glass in the garden. At least they could have organised the children to tidy up, as this was a country where there were no tetanus injections.

I never saw whether the children got to play with any of the toys we had sorted. If I had gone into a room without permission, I would have been put out quickly. I did see a consignment of plastic ducks, but there were no soft toys in the cots.

One doesn't get answers in Romania. It is a different country altogether.

It was not a hopeless situation, though. Rather than give

in to feelings of helplessness, I clung to what I had learned over lunch the day before at Monika's house. The church in Tirgu Mures had a vision for church-orientated social welfare work among the orphans and elderly people. The people I had met from the Isle of Lewis were already raising funds towards a Christian children's home there. In the new home the children would be brought up in a Christian atmosphere, loved and cared for; they could also be adopted into church families to make room for more unwanted children.

I was made aware of the fact that this children's home was the Reformed Church's vision; they wanted to take it on as their responsibility before God. But they needed outside help and advice to achieve their vision. This would have to be done very diplomatically to avoid corrupt officials asking for enormous hand-outs once they learned that outside aid was being provided.

The government's love of bureaucracy meant that the Christians would have to move cautiously. Private enterprise was so new in Romania that it was hard to move without red tape getting in the way. Only the Church or the state could legally own property. I know of Christian organisations which have bought buildings, only to have them revert to the state because they have not met all the prescribed conditions.

For this reason the constitution of the new home had to be exactly right and I spent some time discussing it with Dénes Fulop before I left.

This resulted in Monika's husband Laszlo bringing a second version of the constitution to me in Hungary before we left for Britain so I could begin fund-raising, because I was now so enthusiastic about the project that I knew I should play a part in it. Hearing big, strong men from the church saying, 'We have so many unwanted children – we have to do something about it,' had been very moving. The Christians were prepared to invest much time and energy in the project, probably creating difficulties for themselves by so doing.

Despite the heartache caused by conditions in the state orphanage in which I had worked, there was hope in the new project and the pleasure of meeting fellow Christians and enjoying their hospitality.

All the Christians we met were warm, open people; each day we were invited to someone's home for a meal. I found them a real challenge to my Christian life; Christ came first, and everything else was an appendage. They started every meal with prayer, during which everyone at the table prayed. Even the little ones prayed on their mother's lap. Then they would sing a hymn, psalm or chorus. We could be sitting worshipping for half an hour before starting the meal! Being in touch with such a vital, vibrant church, I felt as if I had gone back to the days of the Acts of the Apostles.

Lunch, at around three p.m. when the men got home from work, was the main meal of the day. They would ensure we had an extra portion of meat and indeed meat and rice were staple parts of their diet. The meat was usually fried, which did not help my cholesterol problem!

Vegetables were non-existent in winter; they just had a few apples that would keep. In summer the land does not yield a sufficient harvest, although there is plenty of arable land, but it seems to be poisoned by chemicals. In the villages everyone has their grapevine and fig trees, and grows their own vegetables – the alternative is to do without. Once the vegetables have grown, they pickle their cucumbers, tomatoes and onions, which taste delicious, but again contain a great deal of oil.

Although they barely had enough pickled vegetables to see themselves through the winter, they would happily use up a big bottle at one meal and reach for another.

They did not have desserts, except for some fruit in summer, but were over-generous with sugar in the rest of their food. I still believe they should be taught what to grow, because carrots and parsnips will keep during the winter. If only a dietician could be employed at their university, the farmers and families could use the land so much better. When I was a child we put our root vegetables into pits, so we were able to dig out potatoes, carrots, swedes and parsnips when we needed them. If that could be done in New Zealand sixty years ago, it can be done in Romania today!

Families who have been to Britain make sure there are vegetables on their table when they return, then find their children are not used to them and refuse to eat them! They drink a lot of herb tea, which they make by gathering leaves in the summer. This saves money, because tea has to be imported. If they have coffee, they drink it Turkish strength, which I am afraid I could not take.

In Hungary my friends went in for delicious fruit soups, but were again fond of frying as much as they could. Even a cauliflower would be broken into florets and fried. It was very tasty, but just not healthy.

On our first Saturday afternoon in Romania, we were taken fifty miles into the country for a barbecued meal near Sovato at a place called Buchin. The autumn colours in Transylvania were breathtakingly beautiful. Leaves on the many broad-leaved trees were not just reddish-brown but all shades of glowing reds, golds and browns. Along with cedars and pines they covered whole hillsides.

It was at Buchin that the Reformed Church had been holding summer Bible camps; horses grazed there and a stream ran through it. It was such a joy to realise that the teaching of the Bible in this land was simply the renewing of a centuries-old tradition.

That was our only 'day off' during the trip. For the past six months the physical pressure of work had been much more intense than I had been used to and had lowered my resistance to infection. That Saturday night we ate in the hotel for the first time and I ate ice cream, which, happily, Helen did not choose. I did not realise it had probably been made with untreated water and spent my first Saturday night in Romania being desperately ill and wondering at times if I would see morning. It was a good thing that Helen had a hearing problem and slept through the night in our shared room; it would have been humiliating to have any kind friend fussing over me.

Perhaps I was too independent in not seeking help sooner. I was reluctant to ask Monika to return some of the tablets I had brought because the believers had so little themselves. I was given some tablets by an American lady in the hotel, but remained dehydrated for some time and never really recovered for the rest of the trip.

At that point Monika put her foot down and insisted I stay with her. Christians in that land would do anything for guests, as I was to discover. One of the things I had taken with me was toilet paper, so on the first night at Monika's house I put a roll in her bathroom. Soon Monika came and told me, 'You didn't need to bring toilet paper. I got some last night.' She had phoned everyone she knew to find out who could give her some. Before that they were using serviettes brought from the West, which were rather better than the cardboard texture of their indigenous toilet paper.

That previous evening Leventi, the young pastor who had had something of a revival amongst his young people when in Tirgu Mures, had visited them and poured scorn over her concern about toilet paper. 'You should be giving thanks you have no toilet paper,' he chided. 'It means that our Bibles aren't being made into toilet rolls!' He was referring to Ceauşescu's practices, which had included having a forty-ton lorryload of Bibles made into toilet rolls!

After the revolution Leventi had been released from exile in a remote area and was teaching in a high school in Cluj, which meant he was in charge of many sixteen-to eighteen-year-olds. At present he is in Edinburgh with his wife and three children to do some reading at the Free Church of Scotland College.

Monika was a considerate nurse and hostess, but I felt rather depleted and spent a few days quietly, taking the opportunity to get to know some of the local Christians, many of whom lived close by in great concrete blocks of flats.

The day before we were due to return to England, an event took place which provided divine confirmation of the need to make the trip.

For a while I had felt an urge to purchase some work by a Romanian Christian artist. By doing so I believed I would be helping to support them. It turned out that Monika knew of one, a woman called Enikö, and arranged for us to visit her apartment.

Once at her block, Helen and I went up to the sixth floor and rang the bell. The door was opened by a very shy young woman who spoke practically no English at all, but understood my request to show me some of her work. She led us into another room where we were confronted with the most enormous oils, many about five foot high, all in brilliant colours and rather like Chagall's work. She was obviously a very gifted artist, but I couldn't see myself coming back to London with one of these enormous works tucked under my arm!

She must have been totally nonplussed when I asked if she had anything smaller, but no, she had nothing smaller in oils.

Did she have anything at all which was smaller, I asked. My concern was more to fulfil this prompting to buy something from her than to hang exactly the right painting on my wall at home.

She was getting ready for an exhibition at the time, but eventually remembered some forgotten works and, climbing up on a chair, brought down from a shelf eight or nine small framed paintings.

There were two that I definitely liked, one featuring symbolic animals in subdued, but delicate colours, and the other what seemed like a man against a background of browns and oranges. Helen agreed to buy the one with the man in it, planning to repeat its vivid colours in a needlework picture.

When I asked the price, the artist hesitated before telling me they were nine thousand *lei* each. That was a bit less than £4.50.

'Oh no, we must pay double,' I insisted.

I still felt I was robbing the woman, because £20 for two framed paintings didn't seem a great deal to me, even though I had no idea what they were worth.

Shortly after ten p.m. that night, Monika received a phone call which seemed to last a very long time. I knew it was the artist on the other end, which Monika confirmed when she returned.

I wanted to know if the artist was unhappy with the amount we had given her.

'No, it wasn't that,' Monika replied. 'She wanted to know who you were, where you had come from, and why you came.'

Having no money left, the artist and her family had been praying that the Lord would meet their needs; there were three children to feed.

So that was why I had been given that overwhelming concern to buy work from a Romanian artist. After all the opposition to my journey, I had had the great privilege of being used to provide this family's needs. If it was only for that reason that I had gone to Romania, it was still absolutely right to have made the journey. God *did* have something for me to do. I felt so humbled and small, yet grateful that God had used me to answer the prayers of this dear Christian family in the middle of Romania. His ways are past understanding. If only we obeyed more often that prompting of God's Holy Spirit to get up and do what we feel God would want us to do. But then we sit back and say, 'Oh, but *I* can't do that! I'm too old and not well enough, I haven't got enough time . . .' I was so glad we had doubled her asking price!

Further evidence of God's grace came to light when Monika asked Enikö to explain what the paintings portrayed. The man crouching at the base of Helen's painting was someone who, knowing he was a sinner, was trying to hide from God. But there is no hiding from God, as the painting showed; the man, curled up into a red and orange ball, was alone in space. High in the sky at the top of the picture was a great, glowing orb. That orb is in much of Enikö's work; it denotes the presence of God. So God was looking straight at this man who was trying in vain to hide:

> Where can I go from your Spirit?
> Or where can I flee from your presence?
> (Psalm 139:7, NKJV)

Helen was now thrilled with her painting. My painting symbolised the sixth day of Creation, when God created the animals of the earth. In swirling mist, two animal representations looked round in bewilderment. Again, in the sky, hung that glowing orb: the presence of God. I love that painting! It has pride of place in my home.

A year later I was invited to dinner with Enikö, her husband Czabo and their three lovely children. I also bought more paintings. Like many of the Hungarian–Romanian Christians, Enikö's family had a real, godly dignity which meant they wanted to give rather than receive, whether it was of the few goods they had or plain warmth and hospitality which seemed to bubble forth from them. Whatever they have is yours. Nobody, least of all Monika, had known they were having a bad time, but they had told God and He had provided.

The episode with the artist ensured that Helen and I returned home with the knowledge that God had used us. What I did not then know was that it was only the first of many confirmations God would use to guide me step by step along His path.

We spent thirteen days in Romania followed by a week back in Hungary with Tamas and Kati. I was still rather wan after the food poisoning, but when Tamas told me we were to be given 'the Party's' old box at the opera for a performance of *Don Pasquale*, I definitely perked up!

The Budapest Opera House is particularly beautiful and had recently been completely redecorated for its one hundredth anniversary. It was quite a moving experience for me to be there, albeit on the wrong side of the curtain, and yes, I did enjoy the performance.

I returned home overwhelmed with gratitude to God for having given me this opportunity to do something for Him, allowing me to meet such committed Christians over there.

I had now also worked inside one of those infamous state-run orphanages and had fresh determination to help found a Christian alternative. It was a small beginning, but with the Lord's wisdom we knew much could be achieved.

On my first Sunday back in church, John welcomed me home from the pulpit and said that he had been wrong even to have entertained fears on my behalf. After the evening service I gave a short talk, telling them briefly about Marta and her miscarriages, the episode with the artist (I had taken my painting along) and of the many dear folk I had met. I poured out my heart about our hopes that we would soon be able to purchase a house to convert into a Christian home for unwanted and orphaned children. Funds had to be raised, and I think I was vaguely surprised that not everyone present ended up with my enthusiasm and commitment!

The congregation of Cole Abbey is involved in many projects and outreaches, and the fact that my commitments were not to be shared by all was a lesson that I had to learn.

I set about trying to communicate the need to raise funds to friends, and many were very interested. We needed about £53,000, so I thought it would be achieved quite quickly, but in the end Romanian inflation defeated us and a great deal more was needed.

However, a new project was to drop through my letter-box, hurling me and Topsy's Children, which had become the name of my charity, in a completely new direction. It was something even more urgent and this time the congregation was to be one hundred per cent behind me! My concern to help the families in need was also to be fulfilled.

5

'Save My Little Son'

When I came back from Romania, I think everyone
assumed I would revert to an orderly, quiet life again,
perhaps getting another dog to replace my little Topsy.
But I couldn't do that, and such news as the birth of
Marta's baby made me all the more determined to go on
helping the people I had met. Having once been used to
help save a young life, who could do otherwise?

I was again spending my time gathering together everything I could get for the orphanage and also for the people
I knew out there, to meet their great needs. I hoped to
fill a lorry, because if one could give Christians good food
and clothing, they would have things to give away and
provide a good witness to their neighbours. This group
of Christians had actually compiled a list of the needy,
not just in Tirgu Mures but in the surrounding villages.
So I knew that any relief I sent would be responsibly
distributed to the right people.

When I gave the talk at church about my trip to
Romania, the one item which had really staggered people
was the episode with the artist, Enikö. They seemed
flabbergasted that an ordinary family's prayers for God's
provision could still be answered with a miracle – these
days you don't often meet people who are praying for their
next meal.

After returning home, I had thrown myself back into
work for Romania but was really quite ill. The time I had
spent with Tamas and Kati in Hungary had been full of
delightful visits from their daughters and grandchildren,

but had hardly left any time to rest. My upset stomach and dehydration had given way to bronchitis and pains in my chest; I did not tell anyone about these until much later when they were actually preventing my doing all the things I wanted to do. I did not mean to be foolhardy in failing to look after myself properly; it was just that the needs of all the people I had met had completely altered my perspective and I wanted God to be able to use me to help them as much as possible.

So on the day I received Dana's letter I had been planning, as usual, how to achieve all that needed to be done in the short day ahead. Reading her cry for help stopped me in my tracks. In an extraordinary circle of connections, it was Monika Szabo who had given Dana my address:

I have two boys and I work with my husband like workers to Iasi. The little boy has one leukaemia and he was treated here in Iasi to the pediadrical clinique. But here we have not drugs and treatments at the high level like in West. I want very mutch save my little son Richard he is 3 years old. I send to you the papers of the hospital in copies. The analises of the blood and the punction of the modular of stem. The last is good there *are not* bad cellules in the modular stem . . .

Now my son is in a little period of remission. I have a little monies only for the transport in the train only. The plane is mutch expensive for us.

I thank you very mutch and I am waiting your answer.

Thank you and Lord blesse you!

With gratitude,

Dana-Florentina Andries.

The same Scripture was uppermost in my mind as it had been on the night I watched the pitiful Romanian orphans on the television and received my call: 'Suffer the little children to come unto me.'

Since hearing those tapes by John Nicholls in 1990, I had known that God had something for me to do in Romania, but I didn't know what it might be. For me there was no joy in hearing that a child had leukaemia, but there was great joy in knowing I might be used to help save that child.

I was praying about Romania every day, and I felt sure, as I still do, that God had got a work for me to do in Romania. It was as strong a call as I had known to Christian work amongst Jews. When you're called to something, it doesn't have to be renewed from time to time; it's part of your life. So if something comes on to my plate, I believe it's from the Lord. I also believe that God prepares us throughout our lives for whatever 'good works (he) prepared in advance for us to do' (Ephesians 2:10).

From the way God had led me thus far, I felt fully equipped for the task of bringing Richard and his mother to Britain and raising the funds for Richard's treatment. I knew it would mean plenty of time and effort, but the Christian life, in my experience, is not one of undiluted joy in daily life. There is spiritual joy from knowing the Lord, which Jesus promised, but in my life I have known sadness and apparent setbacks as well, by giving up some of those things which the world esteems. After I had been converted, I knew it right not only to give up my public singing, but also my engagement to the one man I would have wanted to marry. He was a Jew who would have regarded conversion to Christianity as a betrayal of his race, rather than the fulfilment of biblical prophecy. At the same time I knew that I must not be 'yoked to an unbeliever'. So I have always been aware of Christians' responsibility for their behaviour; after all, our way of life could be the only Bible some people will ever read.

When I was in Romania the previous October I had heard of a child dying of leukaemia; some people connected the high incidence of young leukaemia sufferers with the fact that Iasi was not very far from Chernobyl, the site of Europe's worst ever nuclear accident. My regret at not being able to help those children made me all the more determined to do all I could to help this wee boy.

Accompanying Dana's letter was a brief covering letter from a woman doctor at World Vision, a relief charity, saying the child was curable. (Dana, I later discovered, had turned to World Vision as the only means of getting her letter to me.)

Of course I had to help – if there was anyone else at all available, wouldn't this poor mother have turned to them before she contacted an elderly lady in another land whom she had never met?

This child was of infinite value, and it was a great privilege to be entrusted with his life in this way. If God was in it, He would provide the means and open the doors. So it didn't matter that I was living on a state pension and could not afford a cup of coffee out when I went shopping; the God I serve is faithful and compassionate.

The first thing I did was to phone John Nicholls and explain the latest turn in events which would clearly mean my becoming involved in one little boy's life. He thought I should go ahead with the project.

Next I rang Dr Golden. I had to find out what leukaemia was doing to this little boy and what treatment would be needed; all I knew was that even in the West, children could and did die from the disease, a cancer of the blood.

Dana Andries had enclosed several medical documents with her letter, and a little photo of Richard. Although he had a chubby face, there was a remoteness about his gaze which told me he was suffering.

I had the documents and photo photocopied in a shop near by and took them down to Dr Golden. But when I arrived in the surgery, Dr Golden was more interested in my own health and ignored my important documents until she had thoroughly examined me. After she had diagnosed bronchitis, ordered me to stay indoors for three days and prescribed some much-needed antibiotics and inhalations for my sinuses, I could only be grateful for the fact that

Dana's letter had made me go to the doctor! 'All things
work together for good to them that love God . . .' I
thought to myself (Romans 8:28 AV).

For this little boy the right medicine meant the difference between life and death. And the right place for his
treatment could only be Great Ormond Street Hospital for
Sick Children in London. It was to this famous hospital
that Dr Golden turned for specialist advice. All she could
say to me on this occasion was, 'We'll have to see what
we can do.'

On 22nd February, eight days after I had received
Dana's letter, Dr Golden phoned me with the results of
her investigation. To treat a child at Richard's reported
stage of leukaemia would take two years and cost £10,000.
Six months would have to be spent in Britain, including
periods as an in-patient at Great Ormond Street. There
was a seventy per cent survival rate amongst in-patients,
and only forty-five per cent amongst out-patients, which
they understandably did not recommend.

Meanwhile I discovered some facts about leukaemia
for myself from a Leukaemia Research Fund booklet,
Leukaemia in Children:

'Leukaemia' comes from a Greek word meaning 'white
blood'. The term describes a group of closely related
malignant disorders arising from the immature blood-
forming cells.

All types of blood cells are produced by the bone
marrow. The spongy centre of bones acts as a carefully
controlled factory producing three basic types of cell:
  Red blood cells
  White blood cells
  Platelets
The growth and development of normal cells is
carefully controlled in the bone marrow to produce
the correct number of each type of cell to keep the
body healthy. This production process is extremely
demanding on the bone marrow with about 3 million red

blood cells and 120 thousand white cells being produced
every second. Although there are many different types
of blood cells, these are all produced from a single type
of precursor cell called the *stem cell*.

In leukaemia, the normal control mechanisms in the
bone marrow break down and the bone marrow starts
to produce large numbers of abnormal cells of a single
cell type. The cell type affected is almost always one of
the white cells. These abnormal leukaemic cells begin to
take over the bone marrow and spill out into the blood
stream, the lymph system, and vital organs may become
infiltrated.

The majority of children with leukaemia achieve a
first *remission* with treatment, that is their blood and
bone marrow are restored to normal. This does not
mean, unfortunately, that he or she is cured and that all
the leukaemic cells in the body have been destroyed . . .

Past experience indicates that if treatment was stopped
early at the stage when first remission is achieved,
these few leukaemic cells would eventually multiply
again, and produce obvious signs of the disease once
more. This recurrence of leukaemia after a period
of remission is referred to as *relapse*. Most modern
treatment programmes (*protocols*) are continued for
long periods, e.g. 2–3 years, after remission has been
attained, in order to try to get rid of all the leukaemic
cells in time, and so bring about a cure.

Later I discovered that Richard had acute lymphoblastic
leukaemia (ALL), in common with eighty-five per cent
of children with leukaemia. This meant the disease had
affected the lymphocytes, one of the three types of white
blood cell, all of which are important in fighting infections.
First of all he would need chemotherapy, the term given to
the use of drugs which kill rapidly growing cells. Since they
can affect both leukaemic and normal cells, they have to
be used carefully in correct doses according to the weight
and height of the child.

The good news was that there was a seventy per cent success rate in children treated at Great Ormond Street. The bad news was that before the hospital would agree to treat him, however, it needed more medical information. The documents we had supplied were hopelessly inadequate, merely records of his temperature and other inessential details from a paediatric clinic. Richard would only be accepted for treatment if we could provide a bone marrow aspirate on a clean slide, and his haemoglobin graphs, showing the production of healthy red blood cells.

Dr Golden told me this at five thirty on a Friday afternoon, so I could do nothing about getting the documents until after the weekend.

Getting documents to and from Romania was far from straightforward. When Dana's first letter to me had been returned to her by the Post Office, she was desperate. She had addressed it correctly, including the postcode, but had omitted the road number. What I did not know then was that the letter I received on 15th February had been written in January, when Richard's doctors had sent him home to die for lack of drugs. Through a doctor at Richard's clinic she heard of the British relief charity World Vision, who were working out of Bucharest. So she had posted her important package to them in Bucharest and they forwarded it to their British headquarters in Norfolk, from where it was correctly addressed to me in north-west London!

Realising how time-consuming it could be to post anything directly to Dana, I phoned World Vision to find out if I could use their address again. Sue, a most helpful girl in their UK office, agreed to send faxes for me from Britain to their office in Bucharest. She also put me in touch with Luminiţa, an English-speaking Romanian girl in their Bucharest office, which was certainly God-given, because Dana had no English at all; a friend had written her original letter for her.

So on Monday 25th February I sent a fax to Romania

through World Vision, requesting the bone marrow aspirate and the haemoglobin graphs, which had to be presented in a specific format. After that I was phoning World Vision two or three times a week, but they had not heard anything from Romania, even though they sent repeated faxes. Great Ormond Street were also concerned to know what was happening.

On Sunday night, 17th March, I got a Romanian Christian I knew in London to phone Dana's home and ask why we hadn't got the information. It turned out that Dana and her husband had only received the request on Friday, two days earlier, and she had made an appointment at the clinic for Monday, hoping to get the information down to Bucharest the following Thursday. So the repeated faxes had got lost somewhere in the charity's Bucharest office.

It had taken seven weeks for my request for the correct documents to reach Dana. Luminiţa had known nothing about the faxes, but now I had her number and was able to phone her direct. Richard's graphs did not arrive until 28th March, which was actually my birthday; they were the best birthday present I could have had. The previous ten days had been a great strain; every time I rang Luminiţa, she emphasised how ill the child was, how his mother said he could not stand up but just lay on the floor, refusing to play. (Disease in the bone marrow means that all the bones in a leukaemia child's body can be painful.)

World Vision in Norfolk faxed the graphs direct to Great Ormond Street for me, and I waited until 2nd April for the hospital to come back to me. Only then did I discover that after all they did not have the information which they had asked for; they really needed the bone marrow aspirate, usually made by puncture of the hip bone, with the child under local anaesthetic. The result would be contained on a clean slide, which could be examined under a microscope. But it was not the practice to do such tests in Romania, so I had to hope Great Ormond Street would accept what they had received.

I was working on several levels at once, trying to ensure

Dana and Richard's safe passage by dealing with the
medical and political aspects, and raising funds to ensure
I could actually offer them treatment when they eventually
reached Britain.

As soon as I had received Dana's letter, I had started
to try and raise money for Richard's treatment. From the
whole process of dealing with newspapers and television
and receiving, on Richard's behalf, many generous gifts, I
learnt a great deal about the way different people respond
to the needs of others.

My first step was to get some large sweet jars and attach
a photo of Richard with the slogan, 'Please help save this
child. £10,000 needed.' I put them in near by shops and
doctors' surgeries and, of course, my church. The people
at Cole Abbey were tremendous; there was no doubt that
the sight of this little boy's pale, forlorn face touched
many hearts. Many of those who gave did so sacrificially
– sometimes it seems as if those who can afford it least give
the most! Through my church came the first big donation,
a cheque for £1,000 from the charity fund of Sir Alexander
Graham, the then Lord Mayor of London, to whom John
Nicholls was domestic chaplain. I also received generous
gifts of money from other friends.

But until I contacted my local paper, the *Harrow
Observer*, on 22nd February, the day I received the quote
for Richard's treatment, I could not quite see how all the
money would come in. Happily they expressed interest in
Richard's plight and sent a reporter with a photographer
to interview me. On 28th February, just under two weeks
after I received Dana's letter, they published big photos
of me with Topsy's portrait and of Richard, giving the
full background to Topsy's Children under the headline,
'Little dog who brings hope to lost orphans of the East'. A
sub-heading next to Richard's photo announced, '£10,000
to save the life of this dying boy'. After giving details of
my first trip to Transylvania the previous October, and
reprinting some of Dana's letter, I was quoted as saying,
'Someone said it was too much for him. But that is awful

– how can you put a price on a child's life?' Readers were then invited to send donations to the Richard Andries Fund c/o the *Harrow Observer*. It really was a good article, and started a steady stream of donations, anything from £1 to £20 at a time. There were also some very lovely letters. So although the fund didn't swell overnight, I had proof of people's support.

Sadly, one unbalanced minority felt it was too much for a non-British child's life, and I received some rather distressing, abusive phone calls. Two weeks later, on 14th March, the *Harrow Observer* highlighted this in their 'Comment' column. I had been greatly encouraged by most people's generosity, including a single anonymous donation for £500 shortly after the phone calls, so I was in good spirits when I updated the newspaper. None the less, they were indignant on my behalf and reported,

> It is impossible for any right-thinking individual to understand what kind of person could read of Helen's mission and subject her to this kind of fear . . . No one can say why one man should read about this child and choose to save his life [referring to the £500 cheque] while another attempts to ruin Helen's.
>
> But she is soldiering on, refusing to let one sick mind let Richard die. We could all learn a lesson from her compassion and, if we all reacted to it with a fraction of her humanity, a little boy's life could be saved.

This sort of reporting was wonderfully helpful for Richard, although I honestly felt the compliments were undeserved. God had entrusted me with this work and I was trying to be obedient to Him.

The *Harrow Observer* was really very good to us, because they regularly rang me for updates on my progress and my battles with the authorities in Romania for Richard's medical certificates and records: 'Dying Richard in red tape battle', was their headline for Richard on 21st March when I was waiting for the medical documents.

It all helped keep Richard's cause in the public eye, and the donations were fairly constant. Some of the money was pledged, such as £1,000 from one young family, but I still did not have enough money for airline tickets.

As ever, Norman and Sally were close confidants at almost every step of the way. Towards the end of March a contact of Norman's was able to put me in touch with a man in Cambridge who offered to fly Richard from Iasi to London City airport in his own small plane! This man was bringing another child over from Iasi to Rotterdam on 24th April for heart surgery, so I got in touch with Dana again, this time through a Romanian in the BBC World Service.

'No, he must come sooner,' I heard. 'He is too ill.'

I was also in the process of applying for Richard and Dana's visas. For them to be allowed to leave Romania, I had to send an official invitation to the British Embassy in Bucharest via Luminiţa at World Vision, guaranteeing to accommodate them and pay for Richard's treatment. I did this on 2nd April, the day Great Ormond Street had accepted Richard as a patient. With it I enclosed copies of supportive letters I had received from the Lord Mayor of London and a former cabinet minister, Sir Rhodes Boyson, and a letter from the *Harrow Observer*, saying they were helping to raise money for Richard.

On 3rd April, I had another call from Luminiţa. She had had a visit from Dana and Richard, and Richard was deteriorating; he had just lain on the floor of her office. The sight of Richard's condition must have been distressing for her, because she was very insistent about her main news: the embassy would not issue a visa until they had confirmation that Great Ormond Street was prepared to accept Richard as a patient.

Dr Golden had put me in touch with the haematology and oncology departments at Great Ormond Street, so I phoned Dr Chris Mitchell, who worked for Professor Judith Chessells, the doctor in overall charge of the work with leukaemia children. I explained that Richard was anything but well.

'If he's that ill, it means he's out of remission and in a relapse. We might be able to give him a month or two more. Miss Sinclair, he is surely dying of his leukaemia.'

'Surely something can be done,' I protested.

'No,' I was told. 'You must understand that if he is out of remission *he is dying*.'

I felt my legs give way beneath me. 'I must save this child,' was all I could think. It was a terrible blow.

Straightaway I phoned Luminiţa, asking her to phone Dana in Iasi and tell her to contact her paediatric doctor to establish whether Richard was still in remission.

Next day, 4th April, the message came back, 'Yes, the child is definitely in remission.'

I managed to get hold of Dr Mitchell at three o'clock in the afternoon and repeated the message I had heard.

He agreed at once to fax a letter of confirmation to the British Embassy in Bucharest that afternoon.

By 5th April, the day after Dr Mitchell had faxed his confirmation to the British Embassy, all I had was £2,300, but I needed £2,500 for a deposit on Richard's admission at the hospital. How was I to pay for their air fares? Time was running out for Richard. If I did not get him out of Romania soon, he would die. It was an awesome sense of responsibility.

Since I had previously discovered, to my cost, that one never knew when the Romanian airline's planes would actually take off, I knew it was right to afford a reliable Western airline. On 5th April I wrote to Richard Branson, the chairman of Virgin Airlines, and to other airlines, and at the same time contacted a friend up the road, John Williams, a sensible businessman who often dealt with Austrian Airlines through his electronics business. There were to be no positive replies from any of the others, so it felt as if one of the burdens rolled off me when John announced, on 8th April, that Austrian Airlines would give me free tickets for Richard and Dana if I could arrange publicity for them. They just needed medical certificates to show that Richard was fit to travel.

On 9th April I phoned Luminiţa again, to find out when the embassy was likely to grant the visa so Richard could leave the country. Apparently they usually took up to ten working days. Austrian Airlines were prepared to get Richard out of the country on the weekend of 13th to 14th April, but not knowing if the visas would be ready, I faxed the embassy in Bucharest again, pleading that Richard really was ill and we needed to get him to England urgently. On 12th April Dana was called to the embassy to sign a document, which meant that once again she had to make the slow, expensive fourteen-hour train journey from Iasi to Bucharest. But the result of everyone's efforts ensured that the visas were ready on the fifth working day! And this was the week of Romania's Orthodox Easter, so everything was closed! No doubt the letters from the Lord Mayor and the former cabinet minister had also helped, as well as the *Harrow Observer* faxing letters to British Embassy officials asking them to expedite the visa applications.

I was able to tell Austrian Airlines that we would gladly use their tickets on Sunday 14th April, the day after Richard's fourth birthday. I prayed it would not be his last. The poignancy of the date was highlighted by the *Harrow Observer*, who invited readers to send him welcoming birthday cards.

Richard was booked in to start chemotherapy at Great Ormond Street on the following Wednesday, the earliest date a bed was available, and I felt slightly calmer, knowing that the immediate needs were met. I needed another £200 before the following week, but I was confident this would be made up over the next few days. What I would use to support them after Richard and his mother arrived, only the Lord knew.

My peace did not last long. On Friday 12th April there was another shock. During a last-minute call to Great Ormond Street, I was told that they actually needed a

deposit of £4,000 – rather more than the £2,500 I had
planned for. I had five days to find £1,700! Once again, it
seemed as if Richard's life depended on my determination
to see mountains move! Immediately I started praying and
phoning people again, trying to reach both the people
who would pray with me and those who were possible
benefactors. I had lost count weeks ago of the phone calls
I made to national newspapers, television stations and
charities. I had also written letters until my wrist ached,
but now there was no time for the hesitant approach – all
the work of the past weeks would be for nothing if I failed
to find the money now.

Waiting for people to phone back and trying to reach
those who made the decisions was agonising; I would
explain the circumstances, who I was, what I was doing,
and the fact that Richard was due to arrive in Britain for
vastly expensive treatment in a few days' time, only to be
told that the person I needed was not in the office at the
time. Knowing how much hung in the balance, it was hard
to be courteous at times and I frequently heard my voice
trembling, as I fought the tension that kept me somewhere
between tears and anger.

There was certainly no question of cancelling Richard's
flight, because it was so obvious that God was in it all. I
knew He did not intend me to bring the wee boy thousands
of miles from home only to find there was no money to
cure him.

In between prayers and phone calls, I had a visit
from the London *Evening Standard*, who had latched
on to Richard's story from the *Harrow Observer*, and in
good-sized articles both they and the *Harrow Observer*
mentioned the generosity of Austrian Airlines and of the
well-wishers who had contributed to the fund. The 'human
interest' side of the story was not lost on the *Evening
Standard*; I was pictured holding a teddy donated by
my neighbours while the headline told the world of a
'Spinster's fight to save little Richard'.

In the midst of all my frantic activity, I could not

help thinking it was all quite a change from my former, somewhat reserved, way of life!

However I felt about the sentiments expressed, the coverage was tremendously helpful for letting people know about Richard, because it triggered television coverage. Before the *Evening Standard* published their story about me, I had not got anywhere with national charities or newspapers or television. Although I phoned everyone I could think of, including the TV programme *That's Life*, national newspapers, television channels and charities such as the Romanian Orphanage Appeal and Children in Need, they all regretted they were unable to do anything for Richard. Once the article appeared in the *Evening Standard*, however, all the television stations phoned me! On the Friday and Saturday before Richard arrived, when I had so much to do already, one television company was going out of the door while another was coming up the steep steps to my maisonette! It took a long time, because they all wanted to set up their shots differently and move the furniture around. The BBC and ITV also wanted to film Richard's arrival in Britain, so more arrangements were made.

Of course I had to accept all the publicity gracefully, because it was the only way I could raise money for little Richard's treatment, but I was quite surprised at the small amount that the television coverage yielded.

The one media source of donations which really astounded me came from the kind people who listened to Radio 4's religious affairs programme, *Sunday*; that early morning radio programme with a much smaller audience than TV news programmes brought in more money than all the rest of the coverage put together.

At seven forty-five a.m. on the morning of Richard's arrival, I was in the studio at Bush House.

'Do you think you will manage to raise all the money you need?' the interviewer asked me.

With a half laugh, I replied, 'I'm short of the first down payment to Great Ormond Street Hospital, but the cattle on a thousand hills belong to the Father I trust in. Austrian Airlines have stepped in and they are flying Richard and Dana here today, free of charge, so hopefully I will be able to take the £4,000 into the hospital on Wednesday.'

I could say that in the knowledge that with God all things are possible; I certainly wouldn't want anyone to take on a challenge of this nature without total conviction that it was God's plan and purpose for their life.

As a result of that programme, I heard from friends I'd lost touch with who recognised my voice on the radio, and received some wonderful letters and most generous donations for Richard's treatment, including one gift of £1,000.

That was my last media appearance before Richard's arrival on Sunday night, 14th April 1991. Everything that I could have done had been done. The press were waiting, Great Ormond Street was waiting, and as far as I knew, the rest of the £10,000 needed to treat a child in remission from leukaemia would not be too difficult to raise. I felt that by God's marvellous grace I had negotiated the first hurdles fairly successfully.

What I did not know was that the child I was due to meet at Heathrow Airport *had never been in remission; he had full-blown leukaemia because he had never been treated.*

6

Richard the Lionheart

On the night of Richard and Dana's arrival, Callum
Morrison, one of the Cole Abbey elders, drove me to
Heathrow Airport where I met up with Father Peter
Pufelete, a Romanian Orthodox priest who had kindly
agreed to interpret for me.

Various television reporters turned up with their cameras, continuing the coverage started during the previous
two days. The aptly named Christine Helps of Austrian
Airlines had thoughtfully arranged for us to stand as close
as possible to the exit in the arrivals hall. My guests were
due in at eight fifteen p.m., but the plane was delayed,
so for forty-five minutes we examined all the arrivals,
straining our eyes for the sight of a sick little boy and
his mother.

But before they emerged, two immigration officials
came out to interview me. Was I really going to pay
all their bills and let them stay with me? Patiently, I
explained that the British Embassy had my confirmation.
I could understand Immigration's concern, because they
had already spoken to Dana and she didn't have a penny
to her name, so I explained once again that Dana wouldn't
need any money and that Richard was going into Great
Ormond Street on Wednesday.

From all Luminiţa's reports, I expected to see Richard
carried off the plane, but the first I saw of him was
an excited little boy running around the airport! And
he was bigger than I expected, as he had been on
steroids for a long time. To my bewilderment, he and

Dana actually walked past me, but I thought, 'It must be them!'

Father Pufelete called out to them in Romanian, and they turned round and came back towards us.

There were no words. Dana, a pretty but pale young woman, just hugged and hugged me. I got down and gave Richard the teddy bear from my neighbours, which he silently accepted. He did not know who I was, and just wanted to run all over the place. A great deal of prayer had been said for Richard and his health at Cole Abbey, but this was still the child who had been lying on the floor for months!

Dana was able to offer another explanation. 'Aeroplanes are Richard's passion, and everything here is so different – there is a lot to see.'

The television reporters wanted to know, through Father Pufelete, what Richard most wanted to do. Despite the excitement, he was single-minded. He wanted to go home and have a bath.

As soon as the cameras had stopped rolling, Richard just took off! It was quite funny to see Father Pufelete chasing round the concourse after him, his long black robes flapping.

Callum took us back to my flat, where Richard's excitement increased, if possible, at the sight of all the birthday cards from *Harrow Observer* readers and the toys I had been lent for him, although he kept up his requests for a bath – he did love his baths!

It was now about ten thirty or eleven o'clock at night – a very long day for all of us, but Richard did not want to stop playing with all the toys gathered at one end of the room. He is a bright child; even at that time of night, he was assembling the wooden train set that Norman and Sally had given him and pushing the trains up and down. There were cars and all sorts of other toys and he loved experimenting with them all. Clearly, he had never seen anything to match that array of toys.

Finally we got him upstairs for the famous bath, where

a flotilla of bathtime toys awaited him. These were toys I had kept for other children who came to stay, but Richard loved them so much that he took them all home with him! One day I shall get around to replacing them.

Dana was very happy with the bedroom I had prepared for her and Richard. After discussing it with several friends, I had decided to let them share a room, because Richard was used to all the family sleeping in one room at home. On seeing her room and the bathroom and loo, Dana kept saying the one English word she had learned, 'Clean, clean!' with a beaming face.

Richard had never seen such deep, comfortable beds and bounced happily on them as if they were trampolines. He had been so careful about my furniture until then, that I hadn't the heart to put my foot down.

Dressed in a smart new pair of pyjamas covered in trains which Callum had brought for him, Richard came downstairs for a bedtime snack, but would not touch milk; only a banana was acceptable. In those first few days, I thought that bananas were probably going to bankrupt me before we got him to hospital; he was eating five a day!

With all the excitement, it was a hard job getting Richard to bed. He still didn't look a bit ill; the only signs that he was not a normally healthy little boy were an enormous tummy from all the steroids he had been given at home, and the bruises all over his body.

We finally got Richard to sleep and Dana and I had a quiet cup of tea with Callum before he left.

Later that night, when I was alone once more, I thanked the Lord for bringing this young mother and her sick child safely into my care, and reaffirmed that only He could ensure their future health and safety. The frantic activities of the last few weeks which had occupied me day and night had paid off, and with the knowledge that Richard and Dana were sleeping peacefully next door, I was able to drift off myself.

Having a toddler and a young woman of twenty-five to

stay would, I knew, be difficult; after all, I was over forty years older than Dana, and I was used to living on my own with only dogs for company. I am also fussy in the house; I like everything to be right.

In fact, the difficulties I encountered with a young mother and son in the flat were different from those I had expected.

Communication was not easy at all, because Dana only spoke Romanian. I had tried to learn a little Romanian, and used dictionaries, as well as falling back on the Italian I had exhumed on my first trip to Romania. Dana tried as hard as I did to communicate, but little Richard refused to try to utter a word of English for his first month. Then he seemed to gain confidence overnight, coming down into the kitchen one morning and asking for his breakfast. After that, there was no stopping him! He wanted to know what everything was in English, and seemed almost bilingual by the end of his stay.

Even on his first night with me, though, Richard and I had found no difficulty in communicating over one important issue; after playing with all the toys in the flat, Richard had started jumping all over the furniture! In my most reproving voice I had said, 'No, you mustn't jump on the chairs,' and he had clambered down at once. A negative is a negative in any language!

I had removed some very delicate Victorian ornaments I had around and closed the piano, but one ornament did get broken that first night; a painted egg with the words 'Romania 1990' painted by Helen Gray. It was rather a precious gift from a dear friend, and the delicate ivory stand it rested on was also broken. It was a couple of days before I discovered the pieces, but after that Richard never touched anything. He really was a good child in the way he adjusted to strange food, a strange culture and a strange language.

Dana has a lovely character, and I already admired enormously her determination and courage in fighting for her child's life, but our tastes in food were quite different!

On Monday morning, Dana came down for breakfast
and I soon realised that she expected to have two eggs
a day for Richard and for herself, the usual custom for
most Romanians. There were so many good things that
I could give Richard that I wanted him to try new foods;
for breakfast I wanted him to have cereal and milk and
orange juice, with perhaps scrambled eggs for high tea,
but certainly not two eggs every day.

When it came to lunch, both Dana and Richard cried
when they saw the food I had prepared for them; it
was quite strange to them and they didn't think they
could eat it.

I was very discouraged, because it really was a lovely
meal; a fresh, free-range chicken cooked with lots of fresh
rosemary, mushrooms, broccoli, potatoes and carrots.

'Lord, what am I to do?' I prayed silently.

At about four o'clock Dana decided to fry potatoes,
onions and an egg for Richard instead. When she had
got through a litre of oil in those first three days without
saving any of it to re-use (oil is poor quality in Romania), I
remonstrated. Although my pension didn't run to luxuries,
I was determined to give Richard good food, because I
only had him for six months. I had to try and make fresh
vegetables tasty for him. One charity worker told me that
the courgettes and mushrooms I was buying for Richard
and Dana were too expensive, but what was the point
of bringing them over if I wasn't going to do the job
properly?

'Just give him chips and crisps if he doesn't like anything
else,' a social worker at Great Ormond Street told me.
Richard would have loved to eat chips and crisps every
day, but I went out of my way to fill him up with good
things instead. He would also have loved sweets, but I
drew the line here again because his teeth were rotten
– soon after he had gone into hospital, he had to have
four teeth out under general anaesthetic – an operation
which would not have been necessary with regular dental
check-ups.

So I tried to instil in both Richard and Dana a love for healthy food and talked to Dana about a balanced diet. At home they had been completely shut off from our Western culture with its informative television programmes and mouth-watering cookery books; books of any kind were very hard to come by in Romania.

After their first taste of hospital food, however, my food was much more acceptable! Dana had come over with the idea that everyone in the West was a millionaire, so she was disappointed that I couldn't buy smoked salmon on our first trip to the supermarket. After I had bought lunch for her in the hospital, though, she saw the difference.

In fact, it took Richard just two days to get used to a healthy diet, and he was soon gobbling up six or seven vegetables a day, always starting them before his meat. With all the vitamins and minerals he had been lacking, he grew enormously, and Dana would write down the way I did things to repeat British cooking at home.

During this initial period of adjustment on both sides, I was bolstered by the wonderful letters from people who had heard the *Sunday* radio programme, assuring me of their prayers; I was aware of God's people praying for me all the time. People at Cole Abbey were also praying for all three of us.

Although Richard had arrived the day after his birthday, we had a little birthday party for him. I had bought a birthday cake and my neighbour brought in another along with a new blue suit with an 'I am four' badge for his teddy.

John Williams, who had contacted Austrian Airlines for me, came to see us with his wife, Gabriella, and their children, Francesca and Robert. Although only a year older, Francesca really mothered Richard because she was told he was ill. Her caring attitude did not mean she and Richard were totally quiet, though; the little English girl and Romanian boy became great friends and made lots of noise playing happily.

That Monday we also had Sky Television, ITN and the *Harrow Observer* in my flat. I allowed them all in, partly out of gratitude in the *Harrow Observer*'s case and because I hoped that they would appeal for money for Richard's treatment. Another national tabloid newspaper reporter came to see us and insisted on taking Dana and Richard down to the park in the cold and tried to get them to smile! I couldn't go because I was too busy, which might have avoided the communication difficulties they all experienced; as it was, both my guests ended up in tears.

By contrast, the next day, Tuesday, BBC South-east came and this time I made sure I accompanied them to the park, along with little Francesca and Robert who were visiting again. This time the reporter let Richard take everything at his pace. First of all he was seen chasing a big labrador and putting his arms round it, then I put him on the swing and the camera could show that he was just overjoyed with all the fun provided in a London park. They produced a wonderful programme because they had a happy little boy and his mother.

So by Wednesday Richard had been on London Week-end Television, Thames Television, Sky Television, ITN and BBC South-east. I was too busy to watch most of the broadcasts, but I did hear from friends that only ITN and BBC South-east actually mentioned that I needed money for Richard's treatment. As a result, all the hullabaloo brought in a very small amount of money, which defeated the whole purpose of exposing Richard and Dana to the television. It was very obvious that some were interested in Richard for his own sake and others were simply after a good human-interest story to fill a slot. Happily Sue Lloyd-Roberts of ITN fell into the former category; for her, Richard was not just a news story, but a child in need. She was so good with him, too, and made the point of saying that money was needed. As a result of her appeal, Richard received a cheque for £500. London Weekend Television were also genuinely interested in Richard's case and followed the story faithfully, for which I was to be very grateful.

All the TV reporters mentioned Great Ormond Street Hospital, and I believe they did receive a good amount of money, but it wasn't earmarked for Richard!

At least I now had enough money to pay the £4,000 deposit, which I hadn't had on the day of his arrival, but even after all the press coverage we still needed approximately £6,000 to cover his treatment.

This was somewhat discouraging, along with the abrasive letters which some donors of £5 or £10 sent when they didn't receive an acknowledgement of their gift by return. Keeping proper account books took time, and time was at a premium once Dana and Richard arrived.

On Wednesday, when Richard was to be admitted at Great Ormond Street, I had reluctantly agreed to take Richard to the TV-AM studios early in the morning. Their researcher had rung me repeatedly for a week asking me to take Richard on at breakfast time, assuring me they were the best fund-raisers of all the stations.

For his own sake, I got Richard up at five o'clock in the morning, ready for a car to collect us at six fifteen. We had breakfast at the studio before learning that our interview had been delayed an hour, because the Prime Minister had to be interviewed at Downing Street. At this point Richard rebelled; he went to the loo and had to be cajoled into coming out again – I thought we were going to miss our slot!

When we sat down in the studio, together with a Romanian-speaking journalist specially brought in from BBC World Service, the interviewer said, 'We understand you want to raise money, but we can't do anything about it.'

She was absolutely right, too; apart from a fee for appearing, donations totalled precisely £5! Richard had enjoyed watching the ducks swimming in Camden Lock, but I really didn't feel that compensated for getting a sick child up very early in the morning under what were really false pretences. I later learned that the researcher had been told to get us on the programme at any cost, because Richard provided an exciting story – hence the extravagant promises.

As soon as the interview was over, I took Richard and Dana over to Great Ormond Street, relieved that I could at last pay the £4,000 deposit. Once again we had a pre-arranged meeting with the media. This time it was BBC South-east, who wanted to conclude their film report by showing Richard's arrival at the hospital. We were met by Penny Upritchard, the PR officer, and the hospital administrator.

It was all smiles and handshakes until Richard got through the front door. At that point he dug his heels in and decided he wouldn't go any further! In the end Dana had to pick him up and carry him away, but at least the cameras had caught him marching through the door holding his mummy's hand.

Kind Father Pufelete had given up more of his time to come and translate the doctors' instructions for Dana, and he accompanied us to the seventh floor, where we were shown Richard and Dana's little room.

The sight and smell of the hospital impressed Dana: 'Smells good and clean,' she said approvingly.

Next we met Paul Winyard, the registrar responsible for Richard's treatment. He was a big man with a shaved head; I regret never asking whether the baldness was a mark of empathy with the children in his care! He had a lovely face and was always ready with a story for the children. He picked up Richard, gave him a cuddle and said, 'Now, I'm Paul, and I'm going to look after you.' This was a far cry from my memories of nursing fifty years previously – one wouldn't have dared call a doctor by his Christian name!

Richard was put in his pyjamas and weighed and measured before blood tests were taken.

While we were waiting for the results, I talked to Paul. 'I don't quite know what I've taken on,' I admitted.

'You've taken on a lot,' he replied. 'But children keep you young. You either do or don't love children. And the fact you've brought him here shows you do love children, so he's going to make you much younger and you'll enjoy it!'

'I wish I had your optimism,' I said.

We also met Professor Judith Chessells, who was in charge of the leukaemia work at Great Ormond Street; I was pleased to be able to bring Richard to a hospital which was leading the field in the treatment of childhood leukaemia.

Understandably, she was non-committal at this stage, which was all she could be before she knew more about Richard's condition.

We got the blood test results in half an hour. There was no trace of leukaemia in Richard's blood.

'I don't know what we'll do if there's no leukaemia,' said Paul, 'because he's clearly not healthy.'

I thought, 'What on earth have I brought over?'

The 'acid test' was a bone marrow aspirate. We had the results the following day. It confirmed that Richard had sixty per cent leukaemia in the bone marrow. This was the child who was supposed to have been in remission, but the chilling news was that he had never been in remission. The drugs he had received in Romania had had no effect on the spread of the cancer through his little body.

Paul announced, 'We'll have to start at square one.'

Despair threatened to close in on me again. Richard's leukaemia had gone untreated for twenty months, much longer than was usual for British children admitted for treatment. He would obviously need a full course of treatment, which would have to be paid for somehow. When I told my friends of this latest development, they could not believe that there was yet another obstacle on the path to Richard's cure.

The first few days in hospital passed in a whirl; no one told us a great deal, except that Richard was having his first 'module' of intensive chemotherapy, aimed at inducing remission. He would have another five months later, with continuing drug therapy in between. If this was successful, he would be allowed home to Romania to continue 'maintenance therapy' – more drugs – for eighteen months.

Not until Richard was clear of leukaemia for two years would they be able to say he had been cured, so we wouldn't know the real outlook until April 1993 when he returned to England for a check-up.

I had not realised how involved the treatment was, and resorted once again the booklet *Leukaemia in Children* for the medical facts:

> Chemotherapy is the term given to the use of drugs which kill rapidly growing cells. The drugs used can affect both leukaemic and normal cells, so they have to be used carefully in correct doses according to the height and weight of the child . . .
>
> Examination of the bone marrow is essential for the monitoring of the effects of treatment. It helps the doctor to decide whether changes in the blood are due to the effects of the drugs used in treatment or relapse of the disease and, aside from any changes in the blood, it can provide the first warning of relapse.
>
> Radiotherapy may be used to treat the central nervous system in combination with a course of injections of an anti-leukaemic drug given by lumbar puncture into the cerebro-spinal fluid which surrounds the spinal cord.
>
> A typical treatment programme: the drugs often used are Vincristine and Daunorubicin, both given intravenously (through a vein), Prednisolone (given by mouth) and Asparaginase (given intramuscularly). After induction treatment approximately ninety per cent of children are in complete remission with bone marrow and blood back to normal and many are back to virtually normal health.

So little Richard submitted to five days of intensive chemotherapy, given orally, intravenously and by lumbar puncture (injections into his spine). He endured a great deal, lying in his bed with several tubes going into him and painful injections every day. The ferocity of the drugs also made him sick at the beginning. Dana would try and make him eat, telling him he would die if he didn't, so he swallowed food with tears running down his face. The *Harrow Observer* quoted me as saying, 'There isn't a whimper from him when he has his injections or swallows his medicine, though still the tears are streaming silently. Richard is a fighter, and that raises his chances.'

This was all true, except that he soon changed his mind about the injections! Richard had a horror of needles and began to scream the place down as soon as he saw one. The doctors were not helped by the fact that the steroids he had been given in Romania had broken down some of his veins, and sometimes they had to try three or four places while Dana and I held down this red-faced, bawling little boy. 'There's nothing wrong with his lungs!' they would joke.

After six days, the tripod supporting all the drips going into Richard's body was removed and he was able to sit at the table in the playroom opposite his room and play with one hand while we kept an eye on the other, which still had drips attached.

That first period of eight days in hospital was hard for both Dana and me in different ways. For Dana, there was the uncertainty of a new language and spending all her days and nights in Richard's little cubicle, only getting a walk once a day. During those first ten days, however, Father Pufelete's daughter came in to see her every day and brought Romanian soup, a welcome change from the Peter Pan Cafeteria!

As for me, I made the daily journey between Kenton and Great Ormond Street, which really was exhausting. Since Dana's English was still very limited, I waited, sometimes up to eight hours a day, in case the doctors needed to discuss Richard or change his treatment. I would leave at seven thirty a.m. to be there by eight thirty a.m., bringing in clean clothes for Dana and taking her laundry home again. Once back at the flat in the evening, I had to catch up with shopping and cooking.

I also had to keep a close watch over our limited funds. I had not realised that the hospital charged for treatment by the day; it was £395 per day, an enormous sum, which did not include doctors' attendances and drugs. But the hospital were very understanding about the expense and allowed Richard to come home after that first eight-day module.

After that I had to take him in every day for seven days to receive Asparaginase injections, which reduced to three times a week and finally once a week.

Richard had no objection to his visits because he could play with the toys there; indeed, he had some lessons to learn; he wanted to keep every toy he saw, which didn't make him very popular with the other children at first! Many of the other patients were little Arab boys, whose parents brought them new toys every day. One day, Richard had to be told to give back a brand new, remote-controlled model car! But his behaviour was understandable when one remembered he had simply never had any toys before.

Meanwhile, I felt as if I was trailing into Great Ormond Street all the time! I was saving money by having him as an out-patient, but it still involved taking taxis twice a day, because Richard was often in a neutropenic condition, which meant he was extremely susceptible to infection, and I could not risk him using public transport. Happily Penny Upritchard, the PR officer, was a great source of strength and encouragement to me. The Malcolm Sargent Cancer Fund for Children contacted me and agreed to pay for the taxis and contributed £3 a day towards food. I am afraid that did not cover the amount of food Richard was eating; Dana, too, needed all the food I could give her. When she arrived she was dreadfully thin, almost half-starved.

Good food and the correct treatment brought about such a change in Richard. The steroids had made him prone to great swings of mood. Now, from a solemn, sulky little boy with dull eyes he became a bright-eyed, bouncing child with huge energy.

However, we still didn't have much idea of how Richard was doing, apart from the fact that he had been allowed to come home, until the registrar, Paul Winyard, called us into the visitors' room one day in mid-May. He politely asked the Arab men who were always in there smoking to leave and turned off the incessant television.

'We have the results from the last bone marrow sample we took,' he told us. 'Now it's good news – there's no leukaemia!'

At this I was quite excited, as was Dana when I explained it to her. She got up and hugged me, but Dr Winyard warned us not to get too excited – this was just the start of a two- to three-year treatment, but we could be optimistic.

I was so grateful to God, because Richard had had leukaemia for twenty months and only the most basic treatment, yet his body had responded extremely well to his new treatment. Now I had to leave the outcome in God's hands, knowing Richard was receiving the best possible care. Professor Judith Chessells took a great interest in Richard, while Paul Winyard and another registrar, Jane Pasmore, looked after him beautifully. Paul allowed me to phone him at any time and even gave me his home number. I felt quite desolate when he left for a new post in Philadelphia at the end of August.

One of the most noticeable effects of chemotherapy is hair loss. Richard's hair did not start to come out until he left hospital, and then it was falling into his food and lying in his bed, until Dana took a pair of scissors and snipped away all his remaining hair so he had an evenly bald head. Funny little Richard took it very well and was actually very proud of being bald! I would be mortified if I lost my hair, but he was thrilled to bits! When we took him to the leukaemia clinic later, half the children there were wearing hats, but not Richard! When summer came, though, I felt his head needed protection. So I wrote to Glasgow Rangers, and soon Richard could be seen proudly sporting their team's colours in a cheeky baseball cap and supporter's scarf.

7

Money Miracles

When I first felt God's call to work in Romania, I never dreamt that such great demands would be made of me. There is, perhaps, something rather romantic about driving to Romania under a black velvet sky, in a truck full of much-needed goodies and medicine. But there's nothing romantic about having your nose bitten by a four-year-old when you're trying to catch some sleep, or lying awake at night wondering how to feed three on what is inadequate for one. To be honest, I wouldn't recommend bringing a leukaemic child from Romania to anyone!

Bringing Richard to Britain was a costly business, both financially and emotionally. I had little notion of the uncertainties to come; I simply knew that God had provided so far and would continue to do so. Christ had laid this burden on me, and I had a great concern to convey the Gospel to Dana, to let her know why I had invited them into my home. Although I did not know either of them, my concern for Dana as a whole person was almost as important as my concern for her son.

We continued the previous pattern of regular visits and the monthly injection of Vincristine. I thought everything was going according to plan, until the end of May. By then I was running out of money; apart from Richard's treatment and the extra food, there were basic expenses for Dana like writing paper, stamps and toiletries. One Friday before the end of May I realised I must redouble my efforts to raise funds and rang all the newspapers I had been in contact with before. It was all to no avail;

Richard was no longer a news story. What was I to do?
Meanwhile a real catastrophe was looming . . .

Leukaemic children are particularly vulnerable to infections, because they do not have enough of the blood
cells which fight them. Richard also bruised very easily
– sometimes one only had to touch him for a blue swelling
to appear. I also had to watch his temperature; if he was
bruising badly, it meant the platelets in his blood were
reduced, so at those times I took his temperature twice
a day and tried to prevent him moving about too much.
He also had to be kept away from public places until the
weekly blood tests became more normal.

It was a rising temperature one day at the end of May
which alerted me to the fact that Richard might have
an infection. He kept rubbing his ear, which appeared
swollen. I rang the hospital, told them the symptoms, and
was told to bring him in at once. Thirty-six hours later he
was really ill and receiving antibiotics intravenously.

It was a traumatic time for poor little Richard, because
his mother was unable to visit him. This was because
she was ill herself, and had unwittingly passed on her
infection to her son. For several reasons, Dana's illness
was a catastrophe for the three of us.

All our attention had been focused on Richard, which
was what Dana had wanted. Before Dana left Romania
she had insisted she wanted nothing for herself; it was all
to be for Richard. She was willing to sleep on the street
and go hungry as long as her child was cared for.

Dana's birthday was on Sunday 25th May. I had bought
her a handbag as a present, which I wrapped and left by
her breakfast plate. When she came down, she was listless
and just pushed the parcel aside. I still did not realise quite
how ill she was. She had kept showing me her teeth, which
were not particularly good ones, but as I cannot see a great
deal close up, I did not realise how bad they were.

But when she got up the day after her birthday, her
whole face was swollen. 'Please, please, you *must* do
something,' she implored me.

I took her straight up to Northwick Park Hospital where we waited a long time in Casualty. Finally a doctor saw her, confirmed her temperature was very high, 104 degrees, and said she probably had a bone infection from rotten teeth. One ear was discharging pus, and she was in agony, so we bought some recommended antibiotics. The tablets, together with mouthwashes for her gingivitis from Dr Golden, helped Dana get through a day trip to Cambridgeshire to see friends, but by the day after she was very unwell again and now both ears were discharging pus. Northwick Park Hospital told me to take Dana to Mount Vernon Hospital, which had a dental department. That day I had another appointment to arrange fund-raising for Richard, so Callum Morrison kindly took Dana along, only to be told that she had to be taken to the London Hospital over in East London. As they only saw the first twenty-five patients who were there by eight a.m., Callum and his wife Jean had Dana to stay with them, which was a great help to me. Callum and Dana duly arrived at eight o'clock the next day, but were too late. Next day they were successful in gaining a consultation. Two of Dana's teeth were extracted on the spot and another during a subsequent appointment. They did some other emergency work, but said the rest had to be done privately. This seemed like another setback to me, and I wondered, 'Dear me, am I going to have Dana in a private hospital as well?'

The hospital were also warning that the work would have to be done soon as Dana's teeth were so bad. What was I to do? I couldn't take money out of the funds raised, because they were designated for Richard; using them for anyone else, even his mother, would be a misappropriation of funds. At this point Callum, out of the goodness of his heart, arranged for Dana to be treated at his own dentist. The dentist agreed to do the urgent work, but told us that to put the rest of her mouth right would take weekly appointments for two years. This was really very sad for Dana, especially when I learned that her whole family had clubbed together to pay for her to have dental treatment in Romania. Callum's dentist said that if a British dentist had done any one part of the work in Dana's mouth he would have been struck off the register.

Dana's temporary absence was a challenge for little Richard, who was suffering from his own infection alone in hospital. Every day I visited him and stayed with him until he fell asleep at night. He missed his mother dreadfully and appeared very withdrawn. I would just lift him out of the cot and he would lie on my lap as close as he could. Dana had written out a letter in Romanian which I tried to read to him; it brought a glimmer of interest to his face, but otherwise he was completely lethargic and I became quite depressed about the situation. Not only did I have a sick little boy and his sick mother on my hands, but the daily fees of £395 were rapidly using up what was left of my dwindling funds.

Travelling by tube into the city every day and negotiating all the stairs was also an unaccustomed strain for me, along with the uncertainty of not knowing how long Richard would be in hospital this time, or how I would pay for this infection – something I certainly hadn't banked on.

But seeing him so withdrawn wrung my heart out of me. By that stage I had become so fond of him that there was no way I could face him going back home to die.

By the end of May, I had almost run out of money. It was a rough lesson in the facts of media life. The *Evening Standard*, having written about Richard before his arrival and reported the arrival itself, were not interested when I contacted them now. Richard was, apparently, no longer newsworthy. I tried all the press and TV companies who had been so keen to invade his young life beforehand, but to little avail. Although BBC South-east had been sensitive to Richard's needs in the report they filmed before he went into hospital, they could not do anything for him now.

It so happened that Richard was in hospital at the same

time as eight-year-old Prince William, who had had an accident playing golf at school. When his mother, the Princess of Wales, came to see her son, she visited the other children on his ward, including Richard. The nurses told me she came to see Richard twice, and was really wonderful with the children, but the poor little boy was too sick and miserable to respond to his royal visitor. He wanted Dana, not Diana!

Richard might not have been aware that Princess Diana had visited him, but the press certainly were. Reporters and photographers camped outside the hospital for three days, and I was spotted by a photographer who had previously been to my home.

As a result, one tabloid newspaper began telephoning me at home, demanding a story about Princess Diana. I really did not have time to help with their inquiries, not only because I felt that Prince William deserved privacy, but because I had had such indifferent responses from them when *I* needed help. As the calls persisted, I found it harder to control my feelings.

'Look, I have pleaded with you to help Richard because I'm running out of funds, and I don't even get answers to my letters and calls. And now you have the gall to telephone me to pry on a family in their misadventure. I won't tell you anything.'

'Well, we know Richard's there and you're visiting him. We have our sources,' they replied.

In fact I had recognised some of the same photographers who had been out to my flat when Richard arrived, but had been too tired to speak to any of them because it was after ten o'clock at night when I left each day.

Next they tried another tactic. They would do an appeal for Richard provided I talked to them about the Princess of Wales and Prince William, but there was no way I would do that. There was nothing I could tell them, anyway – I had simply seen the Princess, and her son as he was wheeled by.

'In that case, Richard's life must be forfeit,' I said finally.

I think I was actually crying by that time because they couldn't have cared less about Richard.

This whole interference was an added source of stress for me at a time when I didn't know how I was going to pay the bills and how long Richard would be in hospital. After this exchange I was shaken, and rang Penny Upritchard at Great Ormond Street. She had already advised me to keep a low profile while visiting Richard because the hospital, like me, wanted to protect the royal family. But this time Penny scolded me for even speaking to the press: 'You should have hung up on them.'

'But I haven't told them anything,' I replied. 'All I said was that Richard's life would have to be forfeit.'

Penny was horrified.

'You should never have said that. It'll be headlines – "Prince William in lap of luxury while Romanian child left to die".'

Despite Penny's fears, nothing came of my outburst to that newspaper and the calls stopped after Ronel Lehmann, the PR man for the Malcolm Sargent Cancer Fund for Children, contacted the editor and protested on my behalf.

At last Richard was allowed home. The hospital showed great consideration in allowing me to collect him at eleven thirty in the evening after he had received a blood transfusion rather than the following morning which would have incurred another day's fees. When I arrived, a new, cheerful little boy tore down the corridor to meet me and gave me such a big hug and a kiss – he was thrilled to be coming *home*!

We arrived home at about midnight, but rang Dana at Callum and Jean's so she could reassure him that she would be home soon.

After he had spoken to his mummy on the phone, he was very brave about going to bed on his own without Dana in the next bed. 'I'm not frightened,' he said, waving me away, and put out the light.

The next night it was a different story. He was not going to bed at all, but sat on my knee until he fell asleep. Carrying that well-fed four-year-old upstairs, I thought, 'I can't do this very often at my age!'

He woke up again, so we talked a bit and I read him a story before he fell asleep and I tiptoed back downstairs. Ten minutes later, I heard him crying, so I went back upstairs. This went on several times until I brought him back downstairs and he went to sleep on my knee again. The pattern repeated itself until one o'clock, and it was the same the next night. He wanted to sleep in my bed, but I knew it would become a habit if I allowed it. Besides which, I was exhausted, and when I heard him crying loudly at about four o'clock in the morning, I went in and told him, 'Richard, I've *got* to get some sleep if I'm to look after you. Now I'm going to put the light out and you're to go to sleep! You're a naughty boy!'

There wasn't another peep out of him after that. My heart bled for him, because he was alone without his mother, but I knew I had made the right decision in those unusual circumstances.

Three days later, Dana came home, with her infection cleared up. This was another, wonderful answer to prayer. The antibiotics and dental care had probably saved Dana's life; had she been at home in Romania, without such drugs, she could never have pulled through.

After we had got over the hurdles of their respective infections, I only had the money situation to worry and pray about! Richard's unexpected stay in hospital had used up all the donations from the television programmes and *Sunday* radio programme. Meanwhile, Richard's leukaemia treatment could resume.

It was a Wednesday after his Vincristine injection the day before that I found spots on his head; in fact, one could hardly put a pin between them!

I rang the hospital who advised me to take him to my local doctor. Dr Golden wasn't there, but a locum confirmed my suspicions that this was chicken-pox. He hadn't caught it through exposure to the virus in Britain: rather, it was already in his system because he had had it in Romania.

Jane Pasmore from the hospital rang when I got home: 'You must bring him in immediately. He'll need special drugs.'

'But I haven't any money,' I nearly shouted down the phone.

'Look, it's dangerous,' Jane warned. 'He's *got* to come into hospital.'

'Isn't there something you can let me have to give him at home?' I pleaded. 'I used to be a nurse and won't take any risks.'

She consented at this and prescribed some antibiotics via my doctor.

Arriving at the chemist with Richard's prescription, I received my next shock: the drug needed, Zovirax Acyclovir, would cost £170. My chemist gave me a wonderful discount, because I had already bought so much from him when I went to Romania the previous year, but it was still well over £100.

Running out of money was my worst fear. Now it looked as if it was happening. In desperation I appealed to God again.

'Lord, forgive me, I know I went into this in faith and the cattle on a thousand hills are yours, but what am I going to do if he has to go back into hospital? *Please* help!'

Over a week earlier I had pleaded with the Malcolm Sargent Fund to give me access to the media and they had sent out the medical correspondent and a photographer from the *Mail on Sunday* to interview me. An article duly appeared on Sunday morning, saying that Richard would have to go back to Romania if I didn't have funds. At eight forty-five that morning, before I had even seen a copy of the paper, I had a call from Mark Jordan, a reporter from LWT who had been so helpful to Richard's cause in the beginning.

'This is terrible,' he said. 'Can we do something to help?'

We agreed they would come and talk to me before church that morning. In fact they stayed for the start of the service and their film report showed little bald-headed Richard sitting back listlessly in the pew, gazing round with his lovely big eyes at the praying grown-ups. It was such a poignant scene, and LWT was inundated with phone calls. Once again, though, donations were mostly sent to Great Ormond Street, so by Wednesday, when I discovered the spots, I still didn't have money to pay for any more treatment.

Richard's temperature was normal, but I still took it every hour, praying it would stay down. At least while it was normal, his life was not at risk.

After buying the drugs with the last pounds I had in the Topsy's Children account, I dragged back into the flat and Dana saw my worried face.

'We'll have to start Richard on these tablets right away,' was all I said.

Twenty minutes later the phone rang. It was Ronel Lehmann, the public relations officer for the Malcolm Sargent Fund.

'I've wonderful news,' he said. 'We've got £17,500 for Richard!'

Wonderful news indeed, and what a rebuke for my lack of faith! That morning the doctor had pleaded with me to have Richard admitted to hospital, but I had refused, acting only on my own understanding.

By Friday morning, Richard's temperature was creeping up, although he still seemed well. I rang the hospital, and they told me to bring Richard in as soon as they had a bed free in the infectious diseases ward, which would be after eight o'clock that evening. So I was able to take Richard to where he should have been before, secure in the knowledge that the bills would be met. Nor did I have any real worries for Richard, because I knew all was in God's hands.

Richard was put in a little, hermetically sealed room, denied any visitors except Dana and me. Dana was allowed to sleep in a zed-bed beside him. It was very hard on her, because she could only get out for little walks when he was asleep.

After ten days, Richard was discharged, and I hoped we could settle back into a normal routine. Yet unbelievably, he developed chicken-pox again two weeks later! This time there was no room for him at Great Ormond Street, so they arranged for him to stay at Northwick Park Hospital.

His accommodation was infinitely more luxurious here; our little four-year-old held court in a huge room with his own bathroom and television – quite a change from the tiny cubicles at Great Ormond Street. He was also a great favourite with the nurses, who spoiled him.

Here he had a Hickman line put in, a tube which went straight into the jugular vein, allowing drugs to be administered without the dreaded needles. It had to be removed before he returned to Romania, however, because the risk of infection would be too great.

Ten days later, he was back at home once more. This time I had thirty-six hours' respite before more rashes appeared, rather like shingles with weals. Happily it was much milder this time, so I was allowed to keep him at home. The drugs had to continue, of course, until he was completely better; the bill for the Acyclovir alone came to £515.

One spin-off from the *Mail on Sunday* article was renewed interest from the media who had turned us down a week before. BBC South-east rang up and asked if they could come and film again. I was a bit wiser now, and refused them permission. Undeterred, they showed stills of Richard from the previous film and gave an appeal, using the Malcolm Sargent address, which I thought was wonderful of them. Their two reports brought in about £800 from the general public, which covered two days in hospital. So often I could tell from little notes accompanying gifts that it came from a very old person. Sometimes it was as little as £1, with the apology, 'Sorry I can't give more.' But this was sacrificial giving – £1 on a state pension is like the widow's mite. Someone even dropped a £1 coin wrapped up in paper into Great Ormond Street: 'For the little Romanian boy.' I gave that to Richard as impromptu pocket money for a trip to the zoo. After prolonged consideration, he settled for some juice and a rare packet of crisps. He had realised, even at his tender age, that money didn't grow on trees. When Dana was at the dentist and it was just the two of us, I would try to do something special for Richard, yet he would often demur: 'But it is expensive!'

Richard's three bouts of chicken-pox meant that his second treatment module had to be delayed. This concerned me, because his visa was only valid for six months and applying for an extension could be difficult.

He finally went in for his next module, but his troubles were not over. When he came home again, I noticed after a couple of days that his eyes were bloodshot. Once again, our locum had to phone Great Ormond Street. They were very good again, and told him, 'Take him up to Northwick Park for tests, and phone the doctor who's on call if you're worried at any time.'

The next night, Richard's eyes were swelling and he was complaining that they were sore. His temperature was swinging up and down, so I phoned the doctor at Northwick Park Hospital immediately. Despite his reservations I insisted on taking Richard into hospital and was allowed to return him to the isolation unit where he had been before.

What a shock when I went in to see Richard next day! I found a frightened little boy with a horribly swollen face and gummed-up eyes. Unable to see anything, he was understandably difficult.

I was so sad for poor Dana, because we were both wondering if he would be fit to leave the country when his visa ran out on 13th October, just three and a half weeks away.

He was just as ill the next day, but on the third day, although he still couldn't see, he recognised my voice, held out his hand, and said, 'Come play fishing with me.' So we played fishing, one of his favourite games, in which we used little magnetised fishing lines to 'catch' magnetised fish. He got very excited because with Dana's and my help he was catching all the fish and I only caught an old log from this imaginary pond!

Richard's resilience really was marvellous to behold. His face was swollen still, so he couldn't give the cheeky smile which won everybody over, but he was back in good spirits.

A few days later, the strange infection had gone and his eyes cleared up. After a total of ten days at Northwick Park, he was allowed home in time for his next lumbar puncture and the removal of the Hickman line at Great Ormond Street. They gave him clearance to go home any time after 8th October, shortly before the visas expired.

8

Back to Romania

Towards the end of Richard and Dana's stay in England, we had the very great pleasure of a visit from Dr Monika Szabo, who would be monitoring Richard's treatment at Tirgu Mures when he returned home. It was a joy to see her again, and Dana, who had only spoken to her on the phone before, was thrilled to meet the doctor who was responsible for putting us in touch with each other.

When I brought Monika back from the airport, Richard was in bed, but was allowed down, all smiles and excitement, to meet this kind lady who spoke his language.

Next day, I took Monika to Great Ormond Street, where she met Richard's doctors and learned all she could from them. They were quite impressed at her knowledge of leukaemia, because she had studied every textbook she could find before coming over. Throughout her stay, she divided her time between Great Ormond Street and Northwick Park hospitals.

Dana had a great love for and trust in Monika. One day she came up and put her arms round me and said, 'I am so glad to have Monika. I will phone her every day when I am at home.'

For me, too, it was so good to know that Richard would be in sensible hands when he got home – such a difference from his previous clinic in Iasi, where they thought it not worthwhile to treat leukaemia because it was believed to be incurable.

There was another area where we could see God working: Dana's Christian faith. As she was a Catholic, I had given her the option of attending a Catholic church, but she had insisted she was happy to come to services at Cole Abbey. She never commented much about the services, partly because she did not understand everything that happened, but I believe she was touched by the welcome she received and the general kindness she met there.

As I had a real concern to share with Dana my faith and the reality of Jesus in my life, I'd given her a Romanian Bible on the day she arrived. Although I pointed out where the New Testament was, she wanted to start at the beginning and treat it like a normal book. That meant starting with Genesis and the Old Testament books of the law, rather a heavy diet for someone unaccustomed to Bible reading! After a week I wasn't surprised that the Bible was out of sight and Dana's prayer book back by her bed in hers and Richard's room. Not surprisingly, she said, 'I don't understand it,' so after meals we'd sit down for simple Bible study with a number of Bibles, including a Romanian one.

Once Monika came, however, she was able to be a great help to Dana. Each evening she joined us for our Bible study and it was such a joy to see Dana grasping more all the time. In fact, she had understood much more than I thought and told Monika she had learnt a lot and really was a believer. While Monika was with us, we worked hard at Galatians, because it gives a good basis of Scriptural doctrine, and after her departure Dana wanted to continue spending two hours each evening on her studies, so we progressed to John's Epistles and Acts.

Dana's appetite for Bible study was a real encouragement to me and she clearly grasped more than the basics of the Christian faith. The Bible was becoming a lamp to her path; in addition, she showed real discernment. She loved her church at home, but one night she said to me, 'You know, Miss Helen (that was what she always called me), in my church we have a statue of St Anthony and the people pray to him, but that is wrong. I shall have to talk to our priest when I go home.'

Another night she said to me, 'You know, my husband is a good man and he believes in God, and when I am home for a little while he too will believe like me.'

God will honour her faith, I thought.

Richard also loved church when he was well, because he could play with the other children there. One day he suddenly broke away from his energetic game, came over, put his arms round me and said, 'I am happy! I am playing!'

I nearly cried. He had never been able to take playing for granted because he hadn't had the energy and his legs always hurt. Now he almost always had a big grin on his face. At that moment I knew that even if his treatment was ultimately unsuccessful, the quality of his life was so much better for the time he had left. I thanked God for the privilege of bringing him to Britain.

Richard also met Norman and Sally's children. The two oldest, Jamie and Siggy, had been praying for Richard ever since they knew about him. I had had to delay taking him to see them, because I didn't want him to pick up any more infections.

The effect of the prayer was apparent when Jamie and Richard sat watching a children's video. Jamie had his arm around Richard's shoulders, and Richard's arm was around Jamie's waist. Jamie kept hold of Richard's hand when we took them to a garden centre, where Richard's eyes widened at the sight of all the tropical fish.

On the way out there was a huge selection of sweets, at a 'pick your own' counter. Richard, bless his little heart, had never seen anything like this and helped himself to one. The sweet was quickly in Richard's mouth, and Siggy's protest confused and upset him. Disapproval nearly always made his lower lip tremble. A cuddle and some reassuring words soon comforted him.

During the uncertain, difficult times, Richard provided me with much amusement, not least from his likes and dislikes. Something he adored eating was houmous. One Sunday evening when he was neutropenic, prone to catch any infection, I felt it best that he should stay at home rather than come to church with me, and got Jean to babysit. There was half a pound of houmous in the fridge when I left, which had all gone when I returned – he had eaten the lot! Apart from these occasional excesses, Richard really was quite wise and generally obeyed his mother's and my instructions, accepting that any privations were for his ultimate good. Every twelve weeks, he had to have a lumbar puncture, which required him to go without breakfast, so we made sure he had an extra treat the night before, which was frequently a poached egg on his favourite baked beans. Houmous could never leave the shopping list now; Richard had it every day. However, I did stop leaving out grapes on the dining-room table. We have them in our shops all year round, whereas in Romania they are only available in season, so perhaps I should not have been surprised to find that the two days' supply I bought at ten o'clock in the morning had gone by two o'clock! Dana had been in the habit of indulging Richard because she thought, 'My child is not going to live,' but almost two pounds of grapes after a good meal is rather too much for a wee boy. So I took to hiding the grapes on a top shelf, producing a few at a time for him.

Richard was good about eating most food I put in front of him. The hospital had told me that Weetabix was one of the healthiest breakfasts he could have, and although he didn't like it at first, he ate it manfully and grew to like it.

Richard pursued his interest in food to the kitchen. He loved to sit on the high chair I have in there and question me about my activities: 'What are you doing? When are we going to eat? Smells good!'

After the initial reluctance to learn a new language, there was no stopping Richard once he decided to speak English. He followed me round the flat, constantly asking the names of everything.

Another item which Richard now encountered for the first time was Lego. Callum and Jean Morrison bought him a basic Lego set, and he was entranced with it. He was forever building in his room upstairs and bringing down the latest aeroplane or lorry for approval. With the Lego and planes, trains and cars from different friends, he amassed a huge collection of toys.

He also loved drawing, a talent I felt he had inherited from Dana, who could have trained as a graphic artist. She would draw something and Richard would try to copy it – when Richard later departed with his toy collection, I was left with some lovely drawings. He would come down and say, 'This is for you,' and run away.

Animals enchanted him. If I had the television on in the evening, he would come in and demand, 'Monkeys, monkeys!' He had never seen colour television before and David Attenborough's wildlife programmes were his favourite.

He soon noticed the photo of Topsy I had beside my bed and nearly every day would go round my bed to say, 'Hallo Topsy. I *love* Topsy.'

'I loved her too, Richard,' I replied, and explained that it was because of my love and devotion to Topsy and hers for me that I got involved with Romania in the first place and he was here being made well. At least, we trusted it was a cure.

I shall never forget one afternoon when I was very tired. Richard usually went to bed after lunch and slept two or three hours. I returned to the sitting-room, sank into a chair and shut my eyes. Soon I heard him patter downstairs and enter the sitting-room. 'If I keep my eyes closed, he'll go away,' I thought.

Richard had other ideas. I had taken my shoes off and he started tickling my feet, because I used to pretend I was ticklish. This time I was not pretending, so he climbed up on to my knee instead and started tickling my face. Then, all of a sudden, he bit my nose! I jumped up and cried, 'Richard!' at which he scampered out of the room in alarm. The poor little mite just wanted to have some attention and be loved and cuddled. After I had told

him never to bite my nose again, we made up. Mind
you, I had partly brought that bite on myself, because
one of the many nursery rhymes I taught him was 'Sing
a Song of Sixpence', which ends with a blackbird pecking
off the maid's nose! Having experienced me 'pecking off'
his nose with my fingers a few times, Richard took it up and
was forever running out of the room 'holding' someone's
nose in his hand.

Generally, though, he was considerate of my age and
the fact that I got tired. He would say, 'You tired –
you sleep.' So there was great joy in having Richard at
home, but not much romance.

Dana was far from idle during her stay. When she arrived,
her canvas bag had been full of wool, with just a few
clothes for herself and Richard. She knitted some beautiful
jumpers, all without any pattern and on a circular needle.
Every evening she would sit upstairs and knit jumpers to
sell when she returned home, because the family needed
the money and her absence meant the loss of one source
of income. A lady in our local knitting shop gave her
some Aran wool and she knitted two very nice jumpers
for herself and Eduord, Richard's older brother, and kept
telling me, 'I knit something for you,' but I wouldn't let her
because I knew she would need as much money as possible
once she got home.

Although she was so nimble-fingered, Dana's hands
worried both of us; she was just twenty-six, but all her
fingers were arthritic. She also suffered from arthritis in
other parts of her body; when I took her to buy new
underwear, a definite necessity, she asked first of all for
sensible woollen vests for the winter because she got so
cold and her body ached.

Evenings were one of the happiest times. After our
regular Bible study, Dana would take up her knitting, I
could sit down because I had more or less finished work for
the day, and Richard emerged from his bath to play with
his toys and chatter away to me about all sorts of things.

In our all-female household, he missed his father and brother very much and frequently talked about them. Whatever we went to buy for Richard, I tried to get the same thing for Eduord as well. I couldn't let this little scallywag, Richard, go home with a suitcase full of new things to see a brother who had been neglected for six months. For Eduord, who was six on 11th August, Richard's illness was a big challenge because it affected his life, too. In Dana's absence he had been sent to stay in the country with his grandparents who worked all day out in the fields. What with missing his father, mother and brother, I was very pleased to be able to send Eduord toys via Richard. The church had donated a mountain of Lego and Meccano, which Richard wasn't allowed to open until they got back to Romania, in order that Eduord should be involved as well. People at the church and other friends also gave clothes to Dana, and once again I was touched by the deep wells of kindness in people, waiting to be tapped by the sight of two people in trouble. It is a privilege to come into contact with such goodness in this very sin-sick world.

When the time came to think about returning home, Dana and Richard had loads of new things to pack. People had given them so much. Richard's character and big grin had endeared him to all my local shopkeepers, and they had contributed generously to a collection started by the lady in the sewing shop. I was staggered when she presented me with over one hundred pounds. Several had given him presents in addition to their donations for his treatment; we had to find room for a £25 pair of trainers from the sports shop, and two school bags for him and Eduord. It seemed that Richard melted the hearts of everyone he met.

They were due to leave on Friday 11th October 1991. I had been able to send some cases back by car with a couple from Romania who visited us in September, but I still had to get Dana four new cases. We started packing Dana's

cases early, but were up repacking them until three a.m.
on the previous Thursday, only to discover she would need
two more; she had also filled two big plastic zipped laundry
bags which I was convinced would never be allowed on
board as hand luggage!

Dana and I blinked ourselves awake on the morning of
10th October to find Richard full of anticipation at his
next treat: a trip to RAF station Bentley Priory to see
the Spitfire! Thanks to Flight-Lieutenant Andrew Hill,
a friend from Cole Abbey, and Flight-Lieutenant Gavin
Findlay, the officers and men there had already raised
money for Richard through sponsored events; now they
were going to provide the best farewell gift Richard
could have had. He and Dana would be collected in a
helicopter from Northolt at RAF station Bentley Priory
and flown to the RAF museum in Hendon for a VIP
tour. Once again, I was almost speechless at people's
kindness. The choice of Thursday couldn't have been
better because it would take Richard's mind off his
departure the next day.

So Richard went up in his helicopter, bursting with
happiness and pride. Planes, after all, had been his passion
from the day he arrived. He had thought he was only to
see a plane, but to go up in a helicopter was something
he could not have dreamt of.

When I caught up with them both at the RAF museum,
Richard was totally engrossed by the flashing lights on the
Battle of Britain displays, and tore round happily with
Betsy and Sarah, Andrew's daughters, who were two of
his regular Cole Abbey playmates. By now Richard was
as fluent in English as in Romanian, and he switched easily
from speaking English with the girls to making requests in
Romanian whenever he ran up to Dana.

Other officers and men were exceptionally kind to
Richard, and we returned home with more souvenirs,
including a model plane.

Friday morning came, and Richard arrived in my bedroom

at six a.m. Holding out the new tie he had been given, he said, 'Please,' so I rubbed the sleep from my eyes and tied it. It was a dress Sinclair tartan tie, and Dana wanted him to look his smartest when he went home for his father and brother. I did hope it wasn't the last time he wore it; Dana was unused to tying ties, because hardly anyone in Romania seemed to bother with them.

I tied the tie, and told him, 'Now you're an honorary member of the Sinclair clan.'

As I was tying it, I knelt on one knee and suddenly toppled over. 'Oops, I've lost my balance,' I said.

Quick as a flash, Richard queried the new expression. 'Balance – what is balance?'

So I explained it to him and later, when we were going down the steep steps outside my flat for the last time, he put his little hand out and warned, 'Careful – balance.' He was so quick at picking up English!

John and Gabriella Williams came with their two children and their large car to carry the Andries family luggage, while Donald Morrison, who was driving me, helped load up my car. Believe me, both cars were very full when we eventually set off for Heathrow.

We tottered into the airport with all the cases, which came to 105 kg of excess baggage. To our amazement, Austrian Airlines took it all for nothing! I really cannot speak highly enough of the care we received from them. They told me, 'All that matters is that the little boy is treated and gets well.'

They gave Richard a very lovely porcelain music box in the shape of a grand piano. Richard was entranced to hear Mozart pouring out of this intricate little machine and flattened himself on the floor, lifting the lid to hear the music properly. He was definitely musical, but only the Lord knew whether he would live long enough to develop that gift.

LWT were also at the airport to cover Richard's departure. By now he was well equipped to give an interview in English and enchanted his public by reciting nursery rhymes, thanking everybody for looking after him and blowing a kiss!

Finally it was time for Richard and Dana to walk through the departure gate. We hugged and hugged one another, although we knew it was not farewell for ever, because I was due to fly out myself in five days' time to bring more of Richard's drugs.

But this had been a precious time when three people of quite different ages had come together to save a life and grown to love one another in the process. Saying goodbye was sad, but now I had a daughter, and a grandchild to add to my extended family in Romania. Most importantly, we had won extra time for Richard.

Back at home, I reflected on the events of the last six months. Physically, I had to admit I was burnt out. Looking after two young people was quite a change from looking after little dogs. I had been used to doing things at my own pace, and suddenly I had been thrown into cooking big meals every day and driving far more than usual.

Financially, it had been a greater burden than I ever thought at the outset. Hospital bills alone had exceeded £25,000, let alone all the expenses of food, clothes and petrol.

Yet I had one ringing source of confirmation that I had been right to follow what I believed to be God's leading. If I had listened to the criticism, or taken notice of the opposition, little Richard Andries would have been dead by now. Medically we were not entirely out of the woods yet, because the doctors had given Richard a maximum of five years after the treatment. But he was alive now, and that was God's doing. If I had not met Monika and told her to contact me if I could help in some way, she could not have given my name to Dana. Now Dana was a Christian and Richard had another chance.

I didn't have too long to reflect on what God had done in our lives; preparations for another brief but challenging visit to Romania demanded my attention. Rest and relaxation would have to wait until my return.

9

Answers and Agony

My brief visit to Tirgu Mures on 16th October to take
an eighteen-month supply of Richard's drugs to Monika
was much easier than my first visit a year earlier. This
time I was meeting people who had rapidly become old
friends, and the two days I had allowed were simply not
long enough.

My health was not what it should have been. I knew I
had bronchitis and went prepared with antibiotics, putting
my exhaustion and chest pains down to the bronchial
problems. These were later to be diagnosed as angina.

Monika looked after me very well and encouraged me
to sleep every afternoon, even when we had gone to eat
with friends! The exhaustion meant I could not go and visit
little Richard in Iasi, so I had to content myself with a long
talk on the phone – he hadn't forgotten his English!

Once home again, I promised myself and the doctor that
I would rest. In my mind, though, the practical needs of
the Romanians were flying round again. I wanted to get a
lorryload of food and clothing out to Tirgu Mures before
Christmas; the need was so great. The Christians there
had already identified those in need. Their discipline had
challenged me to the very depths of my being: they had so
little themselves, but wanted to care for these other people
and sought my help in doing so.

In a year, conditions in Romania had deteriorated, and
with inflation at three hundred per cent it was almost
impossible for people to feed their families. Much wisdom
was needed by the people in Tirgu Mures as they applied

for the many permits needed to accomplish the purchase
and conversion of the children's home. Under-the-counter
hand-outs are a way of life in Romania and we did not want
to get caught up in such practices.

I had raised enough money to cover all that I had
agreed to be responsible for in the children's home,
i.e. the children's clothing, the kitchen and the laundry
equipment. A number of other groups were supporting
the children's home project, but my concern was still
for whole families as well as orphaned and abandoned
children. Richard's desperate plight had made me doubly
aware of the urgent need for medical care in Romania,
and my vision of building a basic medical centre there was
becoming more precious.

Richard's impish smile stayed in people's memories, and
constant enquiries about his progress were made by local
shopkeepers, friends and acquaintances.

Many members of the public remembered Richard too.
Unbeknown to me, they had been telephoning LWT to
find out how he was and 'the old lady who had been
looking after him'. On the strength of all the interest, I
received a call from Mark Jordan of LWT one day: they
wanted to do a follow-up Christmas story about Richard.

Were there other children in Romania in Richard's
position, but less fortunate? Mark wanted to know.

'Lots,' I told him. 'The doctor who cared for Dana had to
watch her own grandchild die of leukaemia because there
were no drugs to treat him.'

I could not bring myself to believe that anything would
come of this. A medical centre was such a big project:
how would I ever get it off the ground? But a week
later, the phone rang again. LWT wanted to take me to
Romania and film the whole programme there! When I
had recovered from my disbelief, we arranged that they
would be there to follow Richard from his home in Iasi to
Tirgu Mures for one of his regular lumbar punctures, due
on 19th December 1991. The timing was wonderful for a
Christmas programme.

Once again, prayer was answered and all the preparations fell into place. Hospitals in Iasi and Tirgu Mures were approached: we would not be allowed to film in hospital, but Dana contacted parents with untreated leukaemia children who wished to be interviewed in order to make known the great need for improved medical care in the country.

I was, of course, excited about going to see my wee Richard, and was longing to see his cheeky grin once more. I had missed his hugs very much, as well as his tireless attempts to see if I was ticklish.

So I was setting off to Romania with high hopes, confident that I was going to be in very good company with Mark Jordan, the reporter, and John Sorapure, the cameraman.

Austrian Airlines once again issued free tickets for our return trip from Heathrow to Bucharest. We booked an onward flight to Iasi for the same day with Tarom, the Romanian airline, but also bought tickets for overnight sleepers on the train to Iasi, due to depart at midnight, just in case we were delayed.

Our flight was to leave Heathrow at seven forty-five a.m., and Chrismina, who was to drive me there, came to collect me in good time. On our way, we heard on the radio that there had been an IRA bomb at Clapham that morning. We didn't think it would affect us, but how wrong we were! It took nearly one hour to get from the airport entry to Terminal 2. I rushed inside, with just thirty-five minutes to spare, expecting to find an exasperated Mark and John; but there was nobody waiting for me! I learned later that John had checked in very early with all his camera equipment.

Ten minutes before take-off, Mark rushed in. He had been sitting in a taxi for nearly two and a half hours, and was anything but calm. The desk telephoned to the plane that we were on our way, carrying all our luggage ourselves because it was too late to be checked in. None the less, we were not excused the usual security checks.

I was so glad to see Sylvia Simms of Austrian Airlines waiting at the plane; she helped me get on board, because by this time I was gasping for breath. I have had so much kindness from the staff of Austrian Airlines, and I hope that I will never again be responsible for holding up a plane.

In Vienna, we were asked to wait for two hours instead of the scheduled one hour. This was then extended to four hours, because of fog and deep snow at Bucharest, where the runway lights were also out. We could only hope that they would find an electrician somewhere in Bucharest to fix them. By this time we were becoming anxious about our connecting flight to Iasi, and rightly so; by the time we arrived in Bucharest, three hours late, we had indeed missed it.

With five and a half hours to wait for the train, I suggested we spend the time at the Intercontinental Hotel. When we found a taxi, the boys were introduced to haggling, Romanian style! The driver demanded an astronomical amount of US dollars for the fare, stopping the car in order to browbeat us. When pushed too far, I dig my heels in and refuse to give an inch, so in the end this bandit got less than I would have agreed to pay in the beginning.

Staff at the Intercontinental Hotel were kindness itself, and put a call through to Dana immediately; I was just in time to prevent her going to the airport to meet me. Our luggage was put in a safe place and we were told to make ourselves comfortable in one of the restaurants for the long wait.

We had not been settled long over a cup of coffee when it became apparent that the ladies of the night were hard at work. My two companions were obviously embarrassed, and I was amazed at the women's brazen overtures. When the boys decided to go for a walk around the snowbound city, they padlocked John's camera on to my chair, knowing that I at least would be safe from the working ladies and unlikely to leave the precious equipment.

There were very few people eating or drinking at the bar, so it was easy to notice any change of clientele. Increased activity at the bar caught my attention, and out of curiosity I started watching. A number of African men were exchanging small envelopes for very large wads of notes! Like me, you must draw your own conclusions . . .

But I was not to be left in peace; a man kept coming up behind my chair, rocking it several times in a distinctly unfriendly way. I sat still with what I hoped was a completely expressionless face, praying that the boys would be kept safe and would return soon. I was also moved to plead silently with God for the country of Romania, which I had grown to love.

I could have hugged the boys when they returned. We ordered and enjoyed a good meal, collected our luggage and got a taxi, this time with a helpful driver, to take us to the city's Northern Railway Station.

Stepping out of the taxi into deep snow, I lost a shoe, retrieved it, and walked into the station. Spellbound, I stopped still. In that tired, cold moment, with the smell of steam locomotives carried on the icy air, the great vaulted, leaking ceiling dwarfing the locomotives and the tiny grey figures clutching Christmas trees under their arms, I had stepped back a hundred years. The bleakness of that sight was etched permanently in my memory, making me realise afresh what great problems the country was facing.

Nothing on that journey was conducive to sleep; the train lurched along as if on square wheels, or maybe it was just the frozen snow on the line! Inside it was little better; with no heating and only one blanket, the night took for ever and I gave up the idea of sleep. Long before we reached Iasi I was up and dressed; I also paid a visit to the 'loo', another experience I hope never to repeat.

As the train pulled in to Iasi, I pulled back the curtains to see Dana and her husband waiting. It was a few minutes before six a.m. I banged on the adjoining wall of our cabins, asking Mark and John to hurry because they wanted to film my arrival and wouldn't let me out until John was on the platform with the camera. We did my exit from the train three times, Dana having to greet me each time!

Soon we were at the Andries home for my reunion with Richard. In his hurry to get to the door he bumped his mouth on the upright of his bunk bed (a gift from Topsy's Children), knocking out three of his front teeth! His upper lip was swollen the whole time I was there. I took pains to pay attention to young Eduord, Richard's older brother, because he really had felt bruised at being left for six months. Happily the family was together again, and Eduord now had a brother who could play energetically with him.

Once in the Andries household, I was very glad I had given them good food when I saw what was actually available for a mother like Dana to put on her table. Visiting Iasi for the first time, I was not prepared for the poverty. Conditions were much more severe in Moldavia, of which Iasi is the capital.

Dana would be in the market at four a.m. to search for good, fresh food for her family, but she still could not get milk. Hot water was allowed on three days a week and even then it was turned off at nine p.m. After I had been too late for a shower every night, I could see why Richard prized his baths! Hot water became more readily available early in 1993, and a phone call from Dana in July 1993 told me she could now get good-quality milk. The problem is that extra money must be found to pay for these two luxuries.

It really was very different from Monika's lifestyle in Transylvania, where there was hot water twenty-four hours a day, seven days a week and as much milk as anyone wanted (although it still had to be boiled first).

At least their accommodation was clean, even if it was simple. They only had two rooms, so the whole family slept in one room in order to keep the other as a living-room. They did have bunk beds for the boys, and there was a bed-settee for a guest like me in the living-room, in common with most other Romanian homes.

When I saw Dana's living conditions, I did so wish I could give her more money to cope. She cooked on a two-ring gas stove and her towels were about eighteen square inches and of such poor quality that it rendered them useless. Once home, we made sure towels were soon on their way to Dana. At least Topsy's Children had been able to make it possible for the family to purchase their apartment and make life easier for them in many ways, but there was much more we could do.

Dana had gone to so much trouble to make us welcome, inviting various people to meet us. In a way we were hijacked, as others planned our day. We were interviewed on Romanian television, taken to orphanages and treated with the utmost kindness, but it wasn't what LWT had sent us out for.

Later we did meet some of the people that Dana had contacted – dear, loving parents watching their children die. I don't think I have ever felt so useless or helpless in my life. That night I renewed my commitment to God to do whatever He wanted of me to help these people, no matter how much it hurt.

Next morning we left before six to drive Richard the two hundred miles down to Tirgu Mures for his twelve-weekly lumbar puncture. The road went through the Carpathian mountains and we stopped in a particularly beautiful part for Richard to play in the snow and John to capture the scene for the viewers back home.

The driver of our borrowed car was a friend of Dana's husband, Fabian, and soon identified himself as an agnostic. I asked for his views on the revolution and his reply was something like, 'Before I had enough money to live on, but now I don't.' Then, putting his hand on his heart, he said, 'But I am free and for my children it will be better.' Three weeks earlier he had gone to Timisoara to put flowers on the monument to those who had given their lives for freedom.

Our drive to Tirgu Mures in an aged car took fourteen hours, but once there we were able to relax and, as always, meet others who had come to Monika's home that night to share fellowship and read and pray together. I did not expect Mark and John to join in, but quite forgot about my new Romanian agnostic friend, who was in an Hungarian home for the first time. After we had all prayed, I got up to go to the kitchen, when in a breaking voice our gracious and able driver called on the name of God to show him how he could be obedient! I was surprised, but Monika chided me for my unbelief – they expected the response.

Mark and John stayed with Lidia and Istvan Szabo (no relation to Monika), and spent most of the night asking Istvan questions. Istvan will be the Director of Lidia Home. He and his wife Lidia are tireless workers for the cause of Christ. Lidia's family had suffered much under Ceauşescu, and her father, Pastor Viskay, is one of the most humble and godly Christians I have had the privilege of meeting. Both my travelling companions were much moved by what they saw and heard of the Christians they met in Tirgu Mures.

The day after Richard's lumbar puncture, I went shopping for a Russian hat, which was to be a present for my friends in Lolworth. Both John and Mark were keen to make similar purchases and we were certainly delighted with what we found.

We also visited the house which was to be 'Lidia Home', the Christian orphanage. It was named 'Lidia' after the first Christian in Europe, who opened up her home after the Lord opened her heart (Acts 16). The money for the project had been raised by churches in Holland, Northern Ireland and Scotland, including the Isle of Lewis group, along with Topsy's Children. The Dutch in particular have been very generous to Romania. The sale had only just been agreed, so people were still living there, but I was able to show Mark and John its possibilities as a large, extended family home for around fourteen children from the state orphanages.

The conversion work was due to start in the following spring.

By now Mark and John had seen everything and spoken to everyone necessary for their film, and Mark decided we should fly down to Bucharest the next morning to return to London. Seven flights were scheduled that day, but as each departure time approached, they were cancelled. Eventually Istvan took us to the airport to wait. Mark and John were checked through, but I had to wait in the entrance for a lady to come and frisk me! I noticed tanks out on the runway and a number of 'Antiterrorista' militia with Kalashnikov rifles over their shoulders.

After one and a half hours, a bus arrived with more passengers and a kind lady from that bus checked me through first. The plane came in and was immediately surrounded by the tanks. I cannot say this made me feel safe – quite the opposite, in fact. The atmosphere was full of tension and any false move could have caused a tragedy. No explanation was given for the sudden unrest.

Once on board, we were able to take off, but after nine minutes the stewardess announced that we had to turn back because of bad weather. Our flight back to London that afternoon was now impossible and we faced the dreaded toilets on another train. Could anything else go wrong with travel on this trip?

We landed under the levelled guns of the tanks and once again entered the building. We found that all the phones were out of order and eventually persuaded a senior army officer to let us use the office phone to contact Istvan, who in turn was to alert Austrian Airlines in Bucharest to the situation and tell them we wanted to fly out the following day.

Spoiled Westerners that we are, our expectation was that the bus would take us back to Tirgu Mures where we hoped to get refunds on our fares. We waited – and waited, and waited. Mark was becoming angry and tried hard to get things moving. A Romanian girl standing next to me said, 'But this is Romania; we must wait.'

Eventually Mark exploded. 'There is the bus, there is the driver and here we are – let us go!'

The rifles levelled and I really thought he was going to be arrested. John put his arm around me and simultaneously a sparrow crashed into the plate glass and fell, as dead, to the ground. It was a near wail that escaped me as I cried, 'And now a little sparrow has committed suicide at my feet!' The situation was diffused as all eyes turned to me. My concern for a sparrow utterly dumbfounded everyone, but within five minutes we were all in the bus on our way into Tirgu Mures. Prayer was answered!

Back in Tirgu Mures, it was dark, cold and wet. Mark rushed off immediately to arrange refunds on our tickets. As I got off the bus, I saw Istvan's reassuring figure approaching. Never was a friend so welcome. I fell into his outstretched arms and did not deserve his comment, 'Oh, Helen, you are still smiling.'

We got the last three berths on the overnight train to Bucharest and I found myself sharing a cabin with a cousin of Lidia's. God is good. It also meant that we could have John's camera and all the equipment safely in our cabin, so John could sleep peacefully.

None of us could face the train toilet, so at Bucharest next morning we were in a great hurry to get into a taxi for the airport. Elisabet, my cabin companion, came with us. The driver was a dear man and I asked him how he was managing. I felt so sorry for him, because at that time petrol was very scarce and he said he spent more than half his time waiting in petrol queues, which meant he was unable to earn.

We arrived at the airport at six fifteen a.m. and I rushed in through the snow, wishing I still had my sheepskin boots which I had left in Tirgu Mures, believing someone else's need was greater than mine! I made for the lovely clean loos, but believe it or not, none of them flushed. That was the start of the nightmare.

Other than that there would be no Austrian Airlines flight that day, we could get no information. The weather was atrocious. There were no Tarom planes on the ground, and apparently nothing coming in. All scheduled flights were cancelled. The temperature in the building was below freezing, as were my feet. My medication was running out and I knew I would need it. Hundreds of people were stranded, including an ITN team. I sat with Elisabet guarding the luggage (she was waiting to meet her husband) while the boys tried to gather information.

The boys kept reporting back and Mark purchased three Tarom tickets, even though there was no plane. I knew without a shadow of doubt 'that all things work together for good to them that love God, to them who are called according to his purpose' (Romans 8:28, AV), but for the life of me I couldn't see at that point in time what good could come out of our pickle. With hindsight, I am very glad for the bond which that trip formed between Mark, John and myself.

After some eight hours, we took our luggage down to where we hoped to check in for our Tarom flight. We needed to know if a plane would actually be departing, but the ladies at the check-in desk were built like Russian shot-putters, and Mark's charm did not get him very far. I thought I overheard something about a charter flight going out, but there was a complete blackout on that as well.

Finally we were told we could check in and go through Customs and passport control, but there was no guarantee of a flight out. We pleaded for information about the charter flight (for which our tickets were not valid) and as our luggage was being weighed, our 'shot-putter' said, 'Ask the manager.'

Mark followed hard on her heels and learned that there were three seats available on the charter flight, and they were allotted to us! I could only thank and praise God for His intervention. I don't know how they sorted out the tickets, but we didn't have to purchase more.

There were still many hours to wait. I was too cold to think coherently, but was quietly confident of the eternal truth, 'Can a woman forget her nursing child, and not have compassion on the son of her womb? Surely they may forget, yet I will not forget you. See I have inscribed you on the palms of my hands; your walls are continually before me.' (Isaiah 49:15–16, NKJV). Our flight was the only one out of Bucharest that day.

Arriving at Gatwick late at night instead of Heathrow, we thought that nothing further could go wrong, only to find that the wrong luggage had come with the plane! My case was finally delivered to me at six p.m. on Christmas Eve. I quickly unpacked the Russian hat and headed for the Raynars' house in Lolworth, where I was able to relax, rest and enjoy the company of good friends.

So had this nightmare journey been worthwhile? Most certainly; I had the answers to many of my questions and knew which direction the work of Topsy's Children would take in the future. Having visited Iasi for the first time, I had no further doubts that this poverty-stricken area should have a medical centre. I also had a responsibility to Richard.

The TV programme was broadcast on Boxing Day and certainly stimulated interest. Mark and John had done an excellent job. The scenes of Richard playing so happily in the snow were accompanied by the sound of a church choir in Tirgu Mures singing Hungarian carols. Many of my friends are in that choir, so it was very moving for me in more ways than one. Approximately £4,000 was donated by people who saw that programme, ten times as much as an article in a women's magazine. After all the discomfort we had experienced on that trip, I thanked God once again for His provision. I had given my word to LWT that the money raised would be used solely for the medical centre, and it has now been put towards the cost of the building work.

I was also very hopeful for little Richard's future. He was still on full maintenance therapy after three months back at home – Monika had not had to cut it down and was pleased with his progress.

I only have to think of Richard playing with Eduord to know that I had done the right thing.

10

Rejoicing and Responsibility

On 4th June 1992, I left on another visit to Romania. I had
to take out a drug, Intrathecal Methotrexate, for Richard,
who was due for a lumbar puncture; but I also felt that
this was the right time to research the feasibility of the
medical centre I was dreaming of. There were two people
in particular that I hoped to meet. I had been in touch with
a Professor of Paediatrics in Iasi, and wanted to talk with
her about the medical facilities most urgently needed.

In addition, John Nicholls had drawn my attention to
an interview in the magazine *Christianity Today*. It fea-
tured an inspiring Romanian, Danuţ Manastireanu, who
expressed all my own convictions about the channelling of
aid in his country.

Somehow I felt that this was the man of God's choice for
me to work with in Iasi. The question was: would he feel
the same way? Before we could do anything we needed a
group of reliable men and women on the ground for admin-
istration and advice. Perhaps Danuţ could lead the way.

Stephen Sloan, a solicitor and trustee of Topsy's Children, and his brother Andrew, a surveyor, were to accompany me on this visit. They would work on the 'Lidia'
project in Tirgu Mures with yet another team of men,
mostly from Northern Ireland, who were giving their time
and skills for the Lord's work. I also wanted Stephen to
accompany me to Iasi and be involved in the medical
centre research from the beginning. My health was poor
and I wanted him to know what to do if I should not be
able to continue.

I knew that the conversion work on the 'Lidia Home' was making good progress, although it was a massive job. Hopefully if would be ready to open by the end of July 1993.

The attic had been opened up and yielded a number of single bedrooms, a kitchen, sitting-room and bathroom. I was concerned at the escalating costs and was upset when I learned that the work was to conform to the highest British standards. Alongside any Romanian building, 'Lidia Home' will be very luxurious and from a personal point of view I do not believe this to be good witness – but I believe I am in a minority! The fault does not lie with the Romanians, but solely with the West. I am afraid that we must admit we have a lot still to learn.

After a much more pleasant journey than my previous one, I found the whole Andries family waiting for me at Tirgu Mures, as they had come down from Iasi for Richard's lumbar puncture. The train journey to Tirgu Mures is impossible, so they borrowed a car instead, paying all the fuel costs as well as giving a large donation to the car's owner.

I went to the hospital with Dana – my first time inside a hospital in Romania since foreigners are strongly discouraged from entering them. What I witnessed there cannot be written on these pages. The doctors and nurses could not have been kinder or more caring, but they just had nothing to work with. Even the walls were crumbling!

While I was waiting for Richard to come round after the lumbar puncture, I spent my time with three abandoned babies. The economic situation still had not improved after the years of Ceauşescu, and people still felt they could not afford to feed another mouth.

I also watched a nine-year-old boy dying, very painfully, of his leukaemia. And this was in the hospital in Tirgu Mures: in Iasi there was even less medical care available. Could anyone wonder at my sense of urgency in getting the medical centre established?

My good friends Istvan and Lidia were to drive Stephen

and me to Iasi. I was looking forward to meeting Danuţ, and had made a careful note of his name and address from *Christianity Today*. On discovering, just before we set off for Iasi, that I had left both behind in London, I felt desolate. I could not even recall his full name. Lidia, who had attended Iasi University some fifteen years earlier, assured me that her friends would be eager to help and good would come of it all. None the less, I still made the journey with a heavy heart.

My spirits lifted at the sight of the spectacular summer countryside during our early morning drive. So different to the bleak winter scenes I had found so awe-inspiring on my last visit. Now the countryside was green and so very beautiful: a reminder, if one was needed, that God had brought the land through its winter to a bright new beginning.

We arrived at the Andries apartment for a late lunch on 13th June, and I enjoyed playing with the little boys after eating one of Dana's best meals. Lidia and Istvan went to their own friends after lunch, promising to return at four o'clock to take me to meet the Professor of Paediatrics.

Still upset at the loss of those vital details from *Christianity Today*, my enthusiasm was dampened, but it would not be for long. At four o'clock, Lidia walked in with a smiling man behind her and said: 'Helen, I want you to meet my friend, Danuţ Manastireanu.'

I was amazed. 'But you are the man I have come to meet!' I exclaimed. As soon as I heard his name, I knew it was the same one I had copied out back in London. The words of Isaiah 30:21 rang through my mind: 'Your ears shall hear a word behind you, saying, "This is the way; walk in it . . ." ' (NKJV).

I had made an absent-minded mistake, but God had over-ruled by bringing Danuţ to Dana's apartment. It was wonderful confirmation that I was in the right place at the right time.

We went with Danuţ to meet the Professor of Paediatrics and as Danuţ was bilingual, there was no room for miscomprehension. During our two-hour discussion I found this Professor to be a very caring doctor, as well as being extremely informative. I learned a lot about the health problems in Iasi and, indeed, Moldavia as a whole. I was told that by the time they started school, fifty-seven per cent of children had some degree of disability due to lack of drugs to treat childhood illnesses. Many children had partial deafness and rheumatoid arthritis was prevalent. She sighed, and said she sometimes thought that eighty per cent of the population suffer from it.

Tuberculosis was also rampant, while women were afflicted with infections that have not been heard of in Britain for many decades. Then there were the babies – not only those in state care, but also those whose parents loved them dearly – dying for lack of milk and medicine.

Among the medical supplies I had brought on this trip was a consignment of dried baby milk, and I left everything with Danuţ. I also keep Dana supplied with dried milk, but as we cannot purchase full-cream dried milk in Britain, I have to send her '7 pints', dried skimmed milk with added vegetable fat!

From that meeting, Danuţ, Lidia, Istvan, Stephen and I went straight to another with the council members of 'Filocalia', of which Danuţ is a founder member. Would they want to work with Topsy's Children?

'Filocalia' means a number of things: 'love for truth', 'love for that which is beautiful', 'love for good'. The name had been chosen with care to identify 'the Centre for Christian Studies' which was to be built. It was to operate as an Independent Evangelical Foundation, and to win this right, Danuţ and the other founding members had fought two court cases.

Foundations for a five-storey building were already in the ground. An auditorium for worship seating 250 people would be on the ground floor, along with Sunday school rooms and offices. After much discussion and prayer it was decided that there would be space for a modest medical centre as well!

Under the same roof there was to be a library, bookshop, facilities for making radio and television programmes and for publishing, a section to provide care for young children, and hopefully in the future there was to be a Christian school as well.

I was taken to see the foundations of the complex, which had already received great support from churches in the USA. I learned also of their outreach to the many thousands of university students in the immediate vicinity (Iasi is the second university city in Romania). It would be such a privilege to be connected with this work.

At last my dreams were taking shape. It was marvellous that we had agreed to work together and that the medical centre would be a part of the whole, under the umbrella of Filocalia. Barium plaster for the X-ray room would be the only item we would be called upon to supply directly from the UK. I could now concentrate on raising funds to support the building work and the running of the medical centre. We do have to buy all the equipment as well – it won't run without it. I was so very thankful that the planning and construction work would not be entirely my responsibility now. For several months afterwards I almost hugged myself every time I remembered how that weight had been lifted from my shoulders!

Filocalia would administer the work and there was already a good doctor who was ready to work at the centre full-time when it was open. Once everything was running smoothly, we also wished to have a number of different consultants visiting for ten days or more at a time. They could see patients and hold retraining sessions for local doctors.

The way all the loose ends had come together over-whelmed me. Neither Stephen nor I could remember ever having received so many answers to prayer in one day!

I left Romania this time with a great sense of relief. My vision was becoming a reality, and I was particularly pleased for Richard's sake, because he would be one of the first patients to benefit from the medical centre. In June

1992 he was nearly a year into his maintenance therapy and was due to come off all his drugs in April 1993 when he would have to return to London for a check-up at Great Ormond Street. The long-term prognosis was still not good, but the existence of the medical centre in his home town, coupled with believing prayer, made me more hopeful.

Back in London, I had even more cause to keep on fund-raising. Now I was no longer alone. We arranged for Danuţ and another Filocalia council member, Nelu Chitescu, an engineer who oversees the building work, to come over and help with the fund-raising the following March, when Cole Abbey was holding a weekend conference on mission work. John, the minister, agreed that the Romanian visitors could take part, and I was looking forward to spending more time with them at home.

Fund-raising is a difficult task, and a great deal of money is still needed for the centre. Yet I never cease to be touched by the efforts made by individuals. One young man, Matthew White, executed a sponsored parachute jump for us, and, also in 1992, ran in the Slough Half Marathon with his friend Duncan Leftly. He wrote me a letter afterwards: 'We both managed to finish around the two-hour mark. There were times when I felt like dropping out, but the thought of not collecting the sponsorship money kept me going.'

Matthew has sent Topsy's Children cheques amounting to nearly £1,400. Would that more would do the same to help us!

Early in 1993, a Scottish actor friend, James Cosmo, encouraged me greatly by arranging a meeting with two medical consultants and a business man. I was not sure what would come of the meeting, and arrived somewhat apprehensive, because our rendezvous was Gordon's Bar on the Embankment: Gordon's Bar is the oldest in London. In past centuries the River Thames ran alongside and this 'cellar' was used for storing gunpowder. It still resembles a cellar, but never had more worthwhile plans taken place within its walls. In fact I had never been inside a bar before, and this little adventure was just one more sign of the change of direction my life had taken after years living in the backwaters. Nervously, I took the plans of the Filocalia building and all the relevant information I could lay my hands on.

These men did not need convincing of the needs in Romania, however: they were there because they wanted to help.

Consultant Surgeon Richard Baker had just taken early retirement from Raigmore Hospital in Inverness, and the other medical man was from St George's Hospital, London. John Rutherford was a businessman from West Sussex.

That first meeting lasted six hours as Richard and I sorted out what was needed. All three were so very constructive, and they asked me to arrange another meeting with Danuţ and Nelu when they arrived in two weeks' time, even though it meant Richard flying down especially from Inverness. Yet another answer to prayer was taking shape before my eyes.

My Romanian visitors arrived on Friday 12th March, and we spent Saturday and most of Sunday at the Cole Abbey conference. At four o'clock on the Sunday we left for Cambridge, where Danuţ was due to speak after the evening service at the Cambridge Presbyterian Church. That night we stayed with the Raynars in Lolworth, as the men wanted to spend the next morning at Tyndale House, the distinguished Cambridge library. After seeing it, they decided to plan the library at the Filocalia Centre on the same lines. Their enthusiasm was a blessing to everyone they met, including me! So much was accomplished that weekend.

On Tuesday I was back at Gordon's Bar with Danuţ and Nelu and our three new friends. We made some good progress, because both Danuţ and Nelu were in a position to make decisions on the basis of the advice they received. Richard Baker was going to see a hospital architect who would draw up plans for our floor space, which was strictly limited. As well as the X-ray room and a dark room, there had to be laboratories for biochemistry, bacteriology and haematology, a doctors' consulting room and treatment room. Nelu soon solved one problem by allowing a Sunday school room opposite the consulting room to double as a waiting room. John Rutherford's advice about moveable walls was also invaluable. Again, I had to thank God for all this expert advice that was so freely and enthusiastically given. Each careful discussion and offer of help was bringing this desperately needed medical centre one step closer to reality.

After the flurry of work for the medical centre, the next thing to plan for was Richard's check-up at Great Ormond Street. This time I was determined to bring Eduord over as well as Richard and Dana. The British Embassy in Bucharest granted all three of them visas, so Topsy's Children bought them tickets on Tarom (the Romanian airline) for Friday, 23rd April 1993.

Mark Jordan of LWT was still interested in Richard's story and asked to cover their arrival at Stanstead Airport. It was good to see him again, after the shared horrors of the previous trip.

Stephen Sloan drove me out to meet them – Topsy's Children is certainly well served by its trustees – and we met Mark and a cameraman there. Dana's little family were the last to come through. They all looked tired but very well. When asked, for the benefit of the viewers, what he most wanted to do on his 'holiday', Richard replied, 'To go home for a bath and to go to the zoo.'

On the Tuesday after their arrival the family was more rested when we visited Great Ormond Street. While Dana looked after Eduord, I stayed with Richard when the spinal fluid and bone marrow samples were taken. As the bone marrow appeared in the syringe, it looked quite normal to my amateur eye – the last lot I had seen in 1991 had looked like dirty water full of debris.

When Dana joined us, I felt justified in saying, 'It is good.'

Next day we had to go back to see Dr Ian Hann, Richard's consultant, for the results. Everything was normal.

'He has done remarkably well,' said Dr Hann. 'It is indeed a great pleasure.'

That, of course, was an understatement for Dana and me. After living through the months knowing that some at the hospital thought he would die when he returned to Romania, we were now being assured that he had a seventy-five per cent survival rate which will increase as the years go by – although nobody can have a guarantee of living to old age. If he gets through the next five years clean, it is most unlikely that cancer will recur.

When a young boy has had lymphoblastic leukaemia, doctors watch out for signs of testicular cancer, so Dr Hann told us that a doctor would have to examine Richard every four weeks. Blood counts would also have to be carried out at four-weekly intervals, which the doctor would monitor. On learning this, I had to make arrangements. Richard could not travel to Tirgu Mures to see Monika every four weeks – the twelve-weekly journey for the lumbar puncture was hard enough. If only the medical centre was open! I phoned Dr Vasilache, the Filocalia member who will be in charge of the centre, for advice. At present she lives and practises in Botosani, 120 kilometres from Iasi. She agreed that Dana could bring Richard from Iasi to Botosani for his check-up every four weeks, until her move down to Iasi a few months before the opening of the medical centre.

Should Richard develop testicular or any cancer other than leukaemia, he will return to Britain, as it can be successfully treated. When I asked Richard whether he would like to come back on his own, he answered without hesitation, 'Yes, I'm, a big boy now.'

Dana agreed, saying, 'I would be happy for him to come on his own. He loves you and knows you love him.' Of course, we hope that he will not have to come back.

After the Great Ormond Street visit, Dana, Richard and Eduord stayed with me for four weeks. Dana suspected that the boys' sight was impaired, although they had already been given glasses in Romania. We arranged for them to be seen privately at Barnet Hospital, where they have a very superior eye department, and were shocked to learn that Richard had less than fifty per cent vision and Eduord was not much better. Both boys had serious focusing problems. The glasses they had were of little use and the frames were primitive. We were then advised to get two pairs of glasses for each boy, as any repairs would have to be done in Britain and they would need a spare pair, especially knowing those two active little terrors!

Richard and Eduord now have very practical frames with plastic lenses, and enjoy wearing them! In the short time before they went home, there was an improvement in their sight, so we hope in time that both boys' eyes will be corrected.

After all the medical attention, the boys were free to enjoy a proper holiday. On the first May bank holiday, we all went to Whipsnade Zoo for the day with the Williams family – John and Gabriella, Francesca and Robert. Francesca is Richard's very closest friend; the two of them simply picked up their friendship where they had left off eighteen months earlier. At six years of age I hesitate to use the term 'girlfriend', but they were inseparable, and a lethal mixture together! Happily Robert and Eduord got on like a house on fire.

Richard's energy was beyond belief and Eduord was with him all the way. Just watching those two happy, healthy boys was reward enough for all the effort I had expended in the last two years.

I couldn't keep up with them and had to sit down at the restaurant, knowing that John and Gabriella would take good care of their own and my little family.

The lions and penguins were the boys' favourites; oddly

enough, two new brown bear cubs failed to arouse much interest.

Then came a wonderful day with Mark Jordan at Thorpe Park, the amusement centre in Surrey. I did not expect to enjoy it, but must admit that it was a great day out for all of us. There were lots of places for me to sit while the young folk went on the rides, often plunging over man-made waterfalls with squeals of glee and enjoyable terror. The wetter they became, the more they loved it, and repeated some rides many times.

We spent a long time at the farm. As it was spring, we saw all the young calves, lambs, kids, piglets – even rabbits and chickens! Richard, who adored animals, seemed to share my real pleasure in being with them.

At closing time, on the way back to the car, Eduord started to cry. He had enjoyed the day so much and wanted it to go on for ever. I'm sure I would have felt the same at his age. Next day he wanted to know why they couldn't have a Thorpe Park in Romania.

The next treat was even more attuned to Richard's taste – a day watching the vintage planes go through their paces at the Fighter '93 show held at North Weald Aerodrome not far from my home. It was wonderful seeing the only flying Lancaster overhead and later being escorted by two Spitfires. There were also Hercules and Tornadoes and a helicopter executing aerobatics which I would have thought quite impossible. The trustees made this a family day out and I invited Gavin Findlay to join us. He had arranged so much support for Richard, including the wonderful helicopter flight the day before he went home in October 1991.

The weather was appalling, with cold wind and rain, but the boys loved the planes' aerobatics. Gavin spoiled them, taking them on all the rides and into the side-shows. The boys spent the rest of their time at home making me planes and helicopters with Lego borrowed from Justin, Stephen Sloan's son. I was so glad that they had been able to get out and enjoy themselves, as Richard had not been able to go out to public places much on his last visit for fear of infection.

I knew I would miss them desperately when they went home on 21st May, but kept telling myself that at least I would have unimpeded access to my own bathroom! Nevertheless, I was not prepared for the emptiness of the house when I returned from the airport. I started stripping beds but was so tired that I just lay down on the third one and fell asleep.

Nearly £40,000 has been raised and spent on getting Richard to this point. The money raised by the *Mail on Sunday* is held by the Malcolm Sargent Fund and they reimburse Topsy's Children for Richard's hospital and medical expenses as they occur: so far they have amounted to over £28,000. This includes Richard and Dana's airfares for the 1993 visit, and £1,000 towards the purchase of a much-needed car for the family.

I was legally responsible for all Richard's hospital bills while he was here, so had to pay them first before claiming the money back from the Malcolm Sargent Fund. Dana and Richard also had to be clothed and fed and there were numerous other expenses to cope with. Reimbursements from the Malcolm Sargent Fund were used for these as well as the hospital bills. Later these monies have helped to support the family back in Romania. Dana has been unable to go out to work because of the care Richard needed, and now there is an unemployment problem in Romania, although I hope she will get work with Filocalia in a year or so.

I could never regret bringing Richard to Britain for treatment. Before he and Dana arrived for the first time, I was strong in faith but very naïve. Now I have learned more about their country, I know that the greatest need in Romania is to build up its infrastructure, rather than to concentrate on individual cases. If I had not set out to help save the life of one small boy, however, I would never have moved on to plan the building of a medical centre.

Saving a child's life has also enriched my life through

the love I have received from Dana and Richard, and it was an added joy to find that Eduord also seems to love me as a member of his family. Fabian, his father, hopes to learn English in order to talk to me better.

Now that the medical centre is making progress, we hope to have it open in the summer of 1994. I am convinced that now all my efforts must be channelled into fund-raising for the medical centre alone. (Separate accounts are kept for Richard, the Lidia Home and the medical centre.) Here we take health care for granted: over there, people accept the inevitability of many deaths amongst children. So many lives will be saved once this project is operating properly.

Then there are the older people, whose plight has distressed me beyond words. I would love to be able to open at least two old people's homes in Romania, where the residents could maintain their dignity amidst loving care. This project must wait, however, until the medical centre is open.

Samuel said, 'Thus far the Lord has helped us' (1 Samuel 7:12b, NKJV), and that has also been my experience. More than that, Psalm 23 assures me of God's presence and care for all the days of my life.

I believe that one of the most important things God requires of us is obedience. I find that the hardest of all, but it seems to me that our relationship with Him cannot be right unless we keep striving to be obedient – obedient to His Word, His will and His leading.

God uses His people to evangelise and to help the poor and needy in this sad, troubled world. The qualification for inclusion in the work is obedience, not youth, or even a perfect body. If we truly love our dear Lord, obedience is easier. Is God calling you to do something for Him and you feel you are not equipped? Remember Paul's words: 'And he said to me, "My grace is sufficient for you, for my strength is made perfect in weakness" ' (2 Cor. 12:9, NKJV). Jesus said, 'If anyone desires to come after me, let him deny himself and take up his cross *daily*, and follow me' (Luke 9:23 NKJV). That following may hurt, but I have found that there is no sweeter way.

I would not change places with anybody on this earth. I have been a Christian since I was thirty-five, but these last years have been the most precious and useful of my life. My material goods may have dwindled, but I consider myself richly blessed and among the privileged of this world, because I can say with the psalmist: 'The Lord is *my* shepherd.'

Useful Addresses

Leukaemia Research Fund
43 Great Ormond Street
London WC1N 3JJ
Tel: 071 405 0101

BACUP
3 Bath Place
Rington Street
London EC2A 3JR
Tel: 071 696 9000
     071 696 9003
Information: 071 613 2121

Leukaemia Care Society
14 King Fisher Court
Venny Bridge
Exeter EX4 8JN
Tel: 0392 64848

Malcolm Sargent Cancer Fund for Children
14 Abingdon Road
London W8 6AF
Tel: 071 937 4548

Topsy's Children's Trust
156A Kenton Road
Harrow
Middx HA3 8AZ
Tel: 081 907 9308